AUDITION ARSENAL FOR MEN IN THEIR 20s

101 Monologues by Type,
2 Minutes & Under

AUDITION ARSENAL
FOR MEN IN THEIR 20s

101 Monologues by Type, 2 Minutes & Under

EDITED BY JANET B. MILSTEIN

MONOLOGUE AUDITION SERIES

A Smith and Kraus Book

A Smith and Kraus Book
Published by Smith and Kraus, Inc.
177 Lyme Road, Hanover, NH 03755
www.smithandkraus.com

First Edition: August 2005
10 9 8 7 6 5 4 3 2

Manufactured in the United States of America
Interior Text Design by Julia Gignoux, Freedom Hill Design
Cover Design by Alex Karan of Blaise Graphics, www.blaisegraphics.com

The Library of Congress Cataloging-In-Publication Data
Audition arsenal for men in their 20s : 101 monologues by type, 2 minutes
& under / edited by Janet B. Milstein. —1st ed.
p. cm. — (Monologue audition series)
Includes bibliographical references.
ISBN 1-57525-397-6
1. Monologues. 2. Acting—Auditions. I. Milstein, Janet B. II. Series.

PN2080.A75 2005
812'.045089286—dc22
2005044118

Acknowledgments

I would like to express my deepest gratitude to
Eric Kraus and Marisa Smith for entrusting me with this project
and for their wisdom, patience, and generosity.

I would also like to thank the following people
for their help and support:

Karen Milstein
Barbara Lhota
The Milsteins
Alex Karan
Russ Tutterow
Sandy Shinner
Keith Huff
Karen Vesper
Tom Volo
Julia Gignoux
Susan Moore

All of the wonderful actors who took the time to give their input
and all of the talented writers who shared their work with me.

Contents

ANGRY/FED UP

NERVOUS/AWKWARD/UNEASY

MELODRAMATIC

TROUBLED/PAINED

Audition Arsenal Introduction

Redefining the monologue book

When Eric Kraus approached me about editing a new series of monologue books based on character type, some questions immediately came to mind: Was this type as in theater or film? Most specific types fall under film, yet monologues are rarely used for film or on-camera. For theater there are really only three main types: Leading Man/Lady, Ingénue/Young Man, and Character Actors. If I wanted to offer more detailed types, what criteria would be most useful? Would profession be considered a type? How about funny? Could social status define type?

In addition, I considered what was needed in a monologue book that had not yet been addressed. How would I improve upon the monologue books I own? What would make a book more valuable? How could I create a book to solve the problems my students are constantly voicing? As an actor, writer, and monologue coach, I wanted this new monologue series to give actors what they truly need for auditions. I had my own ideas about what *I* would find useful, but I decided to poll some actors to get their input, as well. The actors had a lot of common requests that confirmed my initial instincts. Most importantly this series would need to maximize the number of monologues an actor would actually use from one source. To do that, the traditional monologue book would need to be reinvented.

How are the books in this series better?

When I was studying acting in college, I'd always wished that there were monologue books just for actors in their twenties. And my dream books would have taken it a step further and been separated by gender to increase the number of monologues in one book that specifically applied to me. Now, I am presenting that to you — Women 20s, Men 20s, Women 30s, and Men 30s. No more skipping over pages and pages because the characters are out of your age range or not for your gender. Within each book, the choices are plentiful, and you're sure to find pieces that fit your specific needs.

That brings me to the next revolutionary feature of the Audition Arsenal series: The books are organized by type. By type, I'm referring to the most prominent quality the monologue reveals about the actor. So instead of being typed somewhat generically (e.g., waitress or Ingénue), the monologues are designed to show you possess the qualities crucial to a particular character or role. Auditioning for a Harry Kondoleon play? Check out the High-strung/Neurotic/Stressed-Out category. Want to get a callback for that Durang play? Prepare one of the Wacky/Quirky/Odd pieces.

Not only can you use these monologues to audition for a specific role, but you can use them to show your range in general auditions. When asked to prepare two contrasting pieces, you can go beyond simply a comedic and a dramatic (or a contemporary and a classical, if requested), and demonstrate significantly contrasting personas. Put yourself in the director's chair. Which would be more interesting to see an actor perform — a blunt, strong comedic piece with a blunt, strong dramatic piece or a vulnerable comedic piece with an intimidating/dangerous dramatic?

As actors, we must remember that directors are often meeting us for the first time and might assume that we can play only what we show them. So by all means show them! Think of the different impressions you make with your classmates versus coworkers, or on a first date versus a job interview. The pieces you choose tell directors something about you and your capabilities. Sell your strengths, cast yourself against your usual type, and prepare your personal "arsenal" of monologues so you'll be ready for any upcoming audition — no matter what it calls for.

Here are some additional bonuses you'll find in this series:

- The monologues are two minutes and under — some are one minute and under — to fit the time constraints of auditions.

- Very few, if any, of the monologues sound classical. Why? If you are required to do a classical and a contemporary monologue, you want them to contrast as much as possible.

- Only a small number of the monologues require dialects or accents. Why? The rule of thumb is to avoid dialect pieces in auditions unless they are specifically requested. If your accent is not dead-on directors tend to focus on the accent rather than the acting.

- There are 101 monologues to choose from in each book!

- The monologues are from plays as opposed to self-contained pieces. Some of the writers, kindly, at my request, edited the pieces slightly or pasted dialogue so that the monologues would be better suited to audition situations. However, when you read the play, you will see the bulk of the monologue in the same form and that the character and his or her situation have not changed.

• I have included a Tips section in each book containing helpful information that pertains to the selection and preparation of monologues.

I hope you find this new monologue series to be as valuable, time-saving, and innovative as I have set out to make it. In this particular book, I anticipate that you'll find a plethora of monologues to use for upcoming auditions. But don't let that stop you from checking out all of the books in the Audition Arsenal series. I wish you the best of luck in all of your endeavors. And when auditioning, have fun and break a leg!

Janet B. Milstein
www.janetmilstein.com

Tips for Selecting and Preparing a Monologue

Selection

Choose monologues that make you laugh, cry, feel, or think: "I can relate to this!" If a piece speaks to you, even it makes you angry, chances are you will naturally be invested in the piece.

Although each monologue in this book falls into your age range, you should still consider whether you could realistically be cast in this role. If not, choose another piece.

Find a piece that helps you shine. When reading a monologue ask yourself if it really shows what you can do or if it sells you short.

If you are selecting a monologue for a specific role in an upcoming audition, be sure the monologue reveals that you possess the crucial qualities needed to play that role.

If you are preparing for generals and are selecting two or more monologues, choose contrasting pieces that effectively demonstrate your range.

The monologues in this book are two minutes and under. However, you may have auditions that ask for two monologues to be performed in three minutes, or for one-minute monologues. When choosing pieces, make sure they fit the requirements. It is not professional to run overtime. In some cases you may even be timed. Therefore, it is best to keep your monologue at least ten seconds shorter than the allotted time slot. Also, keep in mind when you are reading and timing your monologue(s) that performing time will run longer than reading time.

Pick your monologue(s) now! Don't put it off. Choosing a monologue that fits you well, reading the play, and working and memorizing the piece all take time. If you wait until the last minute, you will not be adequately prepared. Unlike cold readings, monologues give you the chance to show what you're capable of when you have time to prepare a piece.

Preparation

In terms of preparing a monologue for use in auditions, there is much work to be done. Depending on where you are in your process and which methods you are studying, you will work differently. However, I find the following steps to be useful regardless of the method you subscribe to and the extent of your acting experience.

Read the play your monologue is from in its entirety. It will help you to understand the character, history, relationship, setting — everything that is needed even when you only perform the monologue. Not only will it help you to clarify your choices and understand the circumstances, but you just might find a new role, play, or author to add to your list of favorites!

If you have difficulty locating the play, look in the permissions section in the back of the book to contact the author or the author's agent to obtain a copy. If that information becomes outdated, check with Smith and Kraus to see if they can help put you in touch with the right person.

Answer the questions below with respect to your monologue and write your answers in the first person (e.g.: I am twenty-eight, I want her to . . .).

Who are you talking to? Make it very specific, not just "a friend" or "Kate." Use the script for clues about your relationship and fill in the rest.

What is your objective (goal, intention, what are you "fighting for")? It must include the other person. What do you want from him or her? Make it specific and bold — go for your dream goal!

When and where is this taking place? Be very specific as it will inform your environment, your body, and much more.

What happened the moment before the monologue begins? What did the other person say or do that compels you to speak the first line (and the rest of your monologue) right now — not two weeks ago, not yesterday, not an hour ago? The moment before is so important. Test it out and fine-tune it until you have chosen something big enough and personal enough to springboard you into the monologue.

Go through the text of your monologue and with a pencil divide the monologue into beats. Look for the major and minor transitions in the text and use your own system to mark them. Do not skip this step or your monologue will likely be on one note.

How are you going to accomplish your objective — achieve your goal? With tactics or actions. These are the things you do to get what you want. When choosing actions or tactics, put them in the form "to verb" the other person. For example: to beg her, to threaten him, to charm her. Go back to your text, think about your objective, and choose an action/tactic for each beat. Test it out, refine it. The text will help you choose. However, be careful not to be so rigid with this process that your monologue loses spontaneity. Over time, you should change your actions if they get stale.

Personalize your monologue. Are there past events, situations, or other characters mentioned in the text? This is one of the most enjoyable parts of the process — let your imagination run wild and fill in the details that are *not* given in the script (but fall under the given circumstances). Be creative and have fun, but don't stop until you create specifics that will live in you fully.

Memorize your monologue inside out and upside down. I recommend memorizing by rote — quickly and without emotion or expression so as not to get stuck in a line reading. The idea is to drill the lines so well that you never have to be *back in your head* thinking about them when you should be *out in front of you* fighting for your objective from the other person.

Work your monologues with a coach, teacher, director, or fellow actor. Auditioning can be intimidating and what we do when performing alone often changes in the presence of others. You cannot be truly focused on achieving your goal if you are trying to direct yourself at the same time. Work with someone who will be supportive yet honest. No matter where we are in our acting careers, we never stop growing and we all need other people to help guide us.

Acting is a shared experience between performers and audience — even when performing monologues. Remember, you may be auditioning by yourself, but you still have an audience and they're rooting for you.

Housing to Share
by Barbara Lhota & Janet B. Milstein

Cal: early twenties

Comic

> *Cal and Dorrine have both gone to a roommate agency to find their perfect match. Dorrine is trying to find a roommate to fit her present apartment. The only problem is that she has control issues, which have driven three roommates away in the past year. Cal is laid-back, but a bit irresponsible. He is trying to find a place where he won't be shot at again and where the roommate is willing to, at least, pay rent regularly.*

CAL: Dog walker? Who said anything about a dog walker? I'm not a dog walker. I'm an animal caretaker. See? There's a difference. Besides, I thought you wanted a roommate who liked your cat — who liked animals? Anyway, that's just part-time really. And I always wash. I have a real job. I'm an actor, but I'm not big-headed or anything. I just do a couple of steady gigs as an actor that bring in the cash. I play Banana Man and Bob the Bear for a balloon-delivery service. I'm considered their best — their top. Can you believe it? Get this. I never even had one acting class. Never. *(Beat.)* You got a cig on ya? *(Beat.)* Ohhh, quit recently, huh? Yeah, I've done that a couple of times. Gets ya cranky. But I can see why you don't like people smokin' here. The walls are so white, no cracks or peeling like my last place. Don't get me wrong. I loved my last place. Really big. Loved my roommate. I woulda stayed there forever if he hadn't shot at me. Yeeahh. *(Her face is full of fear.)* Oh no, it's cool. He didn't mean to or anything. I was just breaking in the window and he mistook me for a burglar. No biggie. I forgot my keys. That's why I was breaking in. And he fired — the gun. It woulda been totally cool. Cause he didn't hit me, but he did kinda shatter the neighbor's stained glass window, so the neighbor sued. And Robby was kinda weird about me ever after, which is cool because I didn't like the mice there anyway. Yeah, one night I woke up and one of them was running across my face. That was it. They have diseases, ya know? Yeah, that's exactly why it's good we'll have a cat here. This is going to be much better. How are the roaches here?

Flight of the Malady
By Adam Simon

Carl: a man in his late twenties who has been hiccupping for over a decade

Seriocomic

> *After hiccupping for more than half his life, Carl is preparing to go on a television talk show to display his awkward malady for everyone to see. He answers practice questions with his wife. This monologue opens the play.*

CARL: The first time, you wonder *(Hiccup.)*; you think "well this is amusing." After a day you think *(Hiccup.)* "Jesus Christ, this can't be right. Someone must've made a mistake *(Hiccup.)* probably the doctors." Surely someone missed something, surely one of them along the way forgot to check the one thing that you're supposed *(Hiccup.)* to check in a case like this. After a year, you start blaming others, at least *(Hiccup.)* you try to. It doesn't work. By five years, you're more or less used to it *(Hiccup.)* like a pair of glasses. It's like your hair color, and those that know you *come* — *(Hiccup.)* come to expect it. Some will even tell you that they find it endearing but you have a hard time believing that . . . *(Hiccup.)*. It's been fourteen now and *(Hiccup.)* I don't think about it. *(Hiccup.)* I no longer *(Hiccup.)* let it interrupt my thought process anymore *(Hiccup.)*. I'm past that. I only think about it when people ask me about it. . . . *(Hiccup.)* . . . does that answer the question?

Limping Towards Babylon
By Julius Galacki

Drunken Grad Assistant, a.k.a. Marcus: mid to late twenties. A dili-
gent, even brilliant anthropology graduate student, but hope-
lessly naïve and lacking in confidence

Comic

> *Drunken Grad Assistant/Marcus has just discovered that his
> advisor and boss, Professor Cleveland Thomas, has appar-
> ently swiped key sections of Marcus' own research. After ini-
> tial resignation, his courage and anger have been unleashed
> by demon alcohol. At two in the morning, he finds himself
> in the front of the professor's house.*

DRUNKEN GRAD ASSISTANT: Your mama has a teapot for a head. Hear
me, you manifesting, documenting bird shit . . . brain . . . thing.
Professor asshole. Yeah. Yeah. I do not like your sentence
sequencing. I will not forget. Will not forget . . . *(He passes out
and wakes up immediately.)* I have not finished! Because, sir. You
are a cheater. A lousy, stealing research consumer. You will not
get away with this. Not, not. Not. Let us . . . recount the charges
of heinous academic cowardice: Number one: You are a coward.
Number two: You had lunch me. [sic] I told you my ideas. And
you listened! Number three: You published "Shamanism: Gift or
Curse?" My title! My title. Number four: You are a scum
sucker . . . Gentlemen of the Jury. You have heard the facts. It is
clear. I find the accused to be an asshole. You may have the
tenure. You may have the wonderful wife . . . the salads at
home . . . and a dog. But you do not have pride. I have pride. I
have dignity. You can take my ideas. You can destroy my public
moment. But I know I was there first. Like Knut Hamsun. Me
and Knut. At the South Pole together. History will remember
your deceit. I will . . . I will . . . piss on your house. I will . . .
puke on your flowers now . . . *(He heads for the bushes . . .)*

Reinventing 007
By Lauren D. Yee

Eugene: early twenties to early thirties, a good-natured loser who dreams of being an actor. He auditions for the role of James Bond, only to be turned down once again.

Comic

EUGENE: " — and the rest is silence." *(Beat, expectant.)* Well? Did you like it? Go ahead. I'm ready for my close-up. What? You want me to come back?! You mean, you'll consider me for the part of — *(Disappointed, as they tell him the truth.)* Oh. The extra. I see. How would I feel about that? How would I *feel* about that?! Are you talking to me? Are you talking to me because I'm mad as hell and I'm not going to take it anymore! Now what we've got here is a failure to communicate because I did not come here to play another fat thug. I coulda been a contenda! You had me at hello when I was going to make you an offer you couldn't refuse, but I don't need no stinking henchmen! So frankly, my dear, I don't give a damn about your ideas on what part I should play because you can't handle the truth that life is a banquet and I would have been your main entree! I was on fire and all you could see was smoke! Did I not make you horny? — yeah, baby? We were going to need a bigger boat! But now . . . *(Teary.)* I just vant to be alone. I'm sorry. I know, there's no crying in action films, but as God is my witness, I'll never play a fat thug again! And one day you'll realize that this could've been the beginning of a beautiful friendship! But you continue casting whomever you want, limiting your horizons, because in the end *(As the Wicked Witch of the West.)* I'll get you, my pretty, and your little dog, too! *(Cackles, then as the Terminator.)* I'll be back. *(Starts exiting, looks back at panel, yells.)* STELLA!

Training My Hands for War
By Matt Di Cintio

Luke: late twenties, cruel and with a heart

Dramatic

> *Luke, a penniless boarder in a small town, has nothing to do*
> *but harass his new neighbors and a young dancer he takes*
> *into his room for brief, torrid encounters. With his rent past*
> *due and the collector outside, he hides in his room. He sits*
> *with a joint in front of the mirror.*

LUKE: I think I feel a midlife crisis coming on. And this is high*ly* unfortunate because I don't feel midlife coming on. Although who's to say? Perhaps I passed midlife years ago without even knowing it. I'm telling you about my potential midlife and its subsequently potential crisis because I feel we may have known each other in the past. You do look terribly familiar — I'm not so sure about the red eyes, the dry eyes, but then again, who's to say? . . . Please, it isn't often I talk to just anybody I see in my bedroom who happens to look familiarly a little like me. — It isn't often I talk to anybody in my bedroom. — I feel I can trust you — with conversation, with banter, witty or otherwise, but also with matters of inscrutable distress. I'm always doing impressions that nobody would recognize. "So I said to my father, after twenty-nine years, You'd better get someone else in that kitchen if she's gonna put shoes on!" Does that sound familiar, do you get it? . . . Do you get this often? That people can trust you? Do people — strangers — like me, I mean, do they approach you and say, "My, aren't you the trustworthy type!" Your face looks like it may have been soft, at one point. I don't get it a lot, much, at all, that I'm trusted, that I look like I can be trusted. That my face is soft. . . . You don't? Come now, tell the truth. . . . No? Swear it. . . . They don't trust you? . . . My, aren't you the trustworthy type. . . . See. Now you've heard it from me. I've changed your life. . . . Would it bother you so much to return the favor?

Mama, Maddy and the Cuckoo
By Dylan Guy

Birdie: twenty, somewhat pigeon-toed, bobs his head very slightly as does a bird.

Seriocomic

> *Birdie has been released by his adoptive sister Maddy, from the description of reality given to him by Mama. Mama found him when he was five and told him he was a bird and she told him the platform upon which he perched was a cage. Maddy convinces Birdie he's not in a cage and he's not a bird. Together, they manage to oust Mama from the house by the end of Act One. In Act Two, Maddy then teaches Birdie to walk and talk. Later, in Act Two, Mama returns in disguise when Birdie is alone and treats Birdie to more crazy babblings. He surprises her when he takes charge and offers counterpoint. He pins her with his verbal intentions and keeps Mama quiet throughout the story thus proving to her that her crazy babblings do not have any affect anymore. Birdie is determined not to let himself or Maddy get trapped by Mama ever again.*

BIRDIE: Now I've got a story for *you*. A young man's father was a butcher and he wanted the son to follow in his footsteps. But the boy was perverse. He actually wanted to choose his own life. Every day after school, the boy had to sweep up the butcher shop, put down fresh sawdust and help cut up the meat. Chop chop, snip snip. Every day was a nightmare, even Sundays, cause his father liked rare roast beef and the boy hated the sight of blood. Then one day, there was a meat shortage and people lined up around the block because his father had the foresight to stock up. Every minute, chop chop, snip snip . . . chop chop snip snip. The crowd got more desperate as they neared the end of the meat supply. The boy begged his father to close up shop. But he wouldn't . . . chop chop, snip snip. Chop chop, snip snip. Then they ran out of meat altogether and the crowd turned ugly. The boy did the only thing possible . . . chop chop, snip snip, chop chop, snip snip . . . Years later neighbors still spoke of the mysterious disappearance of his father. Chop chop, snip snip.

Lives of the Formerly French
By Lauren D. Yee

Gus: male, early twenties to late thirties; a delusional man who thinks he's King Louis XVI of France

Comic

Gus speaks to Jack, a guy on a bench who thinks Gus is crazy.

GUS: I've had lots of lives. Guess who I was in my last life? Come on. Guess. Fine, I'll tell you. But you gotta promise not to tell anyone else. *(Pronounces name with exaggerated French accent.)* Louis. Spelled with an *s*, but you say it like it's an *e*. The French way. Yeah, in my last life, I used to be Louis XVI. See, I was in a theater one day, watching this old movie about the French Revolution. And they bring this guy out 'cause they're going to kill him — Louis XVI. And there I am sitting, eating my Raisinettes and I realize, "Hey! That's *me* they're beheading!" The truth hit me so hard I didn't wake up until they let me out of the hospital two weeks later. Said I'd gone insane. Insane with the truth is what I say. And I'm not the only formerly French one. I found my wife. *(Expectant, beat.)* It's you, blockhead! You're Marie Antoinette. So what if you don't remember? Lots of people don't remember things. Maybe you've got one of those repressive memories, where you block out stuff, don't ya think? Don't leave. It took me years to find you and now you're just going to leave? C'mon! You don't know if there's such a thing as reincarnation or not, do you? And if there is, you must have been someone before, right? You see, that's exactly what I mean. You don't know for one-hundred-God-forsaken-kick-the-bucket-percent sure, but then you can't rule it out all the way. I mean, you must have been *someone* before you were you. Marie Antoinette was someone. And if I'm not Louis XVI and you're not Marie Antoinette, then how come we're both sitting at this bench? Isn't it a little too convenient that both of us just *happened* to pick this here bench on this particular day and just *happened* to sit next to each other? So couldn't we be the reincarnations of French royalty who just *happened* to get bumped off two hundred years ago? *(Beat.)* Oh, Marie, I knew you'd remember!

All Things Chicken
By Julius Galacki

Dave Shipman: mid-twenties; smaller in size than his friend Ray; a charming nudge, a manipulative angel; Ray's equal and opposite

Seriocomic

> *In this scene, Dave and Ray are on a climactic road trip to find a place far from city lights in order to view a once-in-a-lifetime visit by a comet. Dave, who has exhibited an extraordinary degree of self-centeredness throughout the play, is partially motivated by boredom but also to do something to get his buddy out of a severe depression. He surprises Ray, and perhaps himself, by revealing — with bravado — some vulnerable truths to Ray for the very first time.*

DAVE: Smell that? Smells like childhood. . . . Not *just* hay. Childhood. We used to ride horses at boarding school. . . . I told you. . . . Yes, I did. I've got facets too. *(Strangely cheerful.)* Yep, I'm the product of a dysfunctional divorce. . . . But I can't think about that. I'm getting along with my father much better now. He's making up for all the terrible things he did. . . . We didn't go on trips. We didn't go to the zoo. All the things you're supposed to do with your kids. . . . Well, when I was six, he did buy me sparklers whenever he went to New York for his weekly acupuncture treatment. But when his back got better, that stopped. . . . Actually boarding school wasn't so bad. There was always someone around. There was no way you could get bored. They made your schedule for you. Class time. Lunchtime. Riding time. Dinnertime. Sleep time. And it didn't matter how much you fucked off in class, because you couldn't get kicked out as long as they got your money. And there was always someone to eat with. . . . Yep. Things are getting better and better. Better and better. My arrow is going in the right direction. . . . Look, there's a fish place. Lobsters: nine, ninety-five.

Moving Picture
By Dan O'Brien

Fred Ott: twenties to early thirties

Dramatic

> *Fred Ott, an engineer in Thomas Edison's laboratory, is defending the limits of his own talent and ambition to a more talented and ambitious co-worker.*

OTT: Do you know what it's like to realize you'll never do anything remarkable with your life? It's liberating. . . . But you're right: really missed my calling. Should've been an actor. Not one of your Shakespeare blowhards. A man of the people's theater, the voe-dee-veal: a dancing monkey, or a singer — one of the ethnic comics. You should hear my Yiddish. You should see me in blackface. That's where my talent truly lies — making people laugh. I worked for a summer at a theater in the country when I was young. — Have I told you this? I was playing a woodland sprite. My father was in the audience one night, and afterwards he came backstage and looked at me in my green tights: "We'll have to find you an older man," he said. You see, because I hadn't any money. And because of my green tights. So I chucked the stage and started making things for other people . . . I'm telling you this so it won't happen to you.

Mars Needs Women, but Not as Much as Arnold Schecter
By Rich Orloff

J. D.: twenties

Comic

> J. D., *who thinks he's a gift to women, is trying to console his friend Arnold, who recently lost his girlfriend to a Martian.*

J. D.: Women, they're so surface. They say *we're* surface, but they're the ones who are surface. We may fantasize about making love to tantalizing women whose firm, delicious bodies make our glands charge into overdrive, but when push comes to shove, we'll screw anyone. We don't have the arrogance women have. Last night, I went out with this chick. Now it's not like it's the first date or nothing that I'm putting the moves on her. It's already the second date; third, if you count the time I drove her to the foot doctor. So I take her out to a fancy restaurant, you know, with tablecloths, and when we're done eating, and I let her finish, I pick up the tab, leave a nice tip, 11.6 percent, and then we go to a first-run movie, and I buy this expensive tub of popcorn, and I don't even care how much she's having — roughly two-fifths, and then after the movie we go out and I buy her a couple of drinks, the fancy kind, with those cherries that give you cancer, and then I take her back to her place, and I tell her she's beautiful, beautiful, *beautiful*, and then she says, get this, she says she's still not ready to have sex with me. And I'm so stunned, I just blurt out, "What do women want?" And she says, "I like my popcorn *buttered*."

Eleven Southern Spices
By Justin Warner

Clark: twenties to thirties, a romantic, Clark Gable–like temporary
stock boy at a fast-food Fried chicken joint

Comic

> *Clark, an old-fashioned, young, romantic Southern gentle-*
> *man, is working a temp job at a fast-food restaurant off the*
> *New Jersey Turnpike. He is smitten by Sylvia, a short-order*
> *cook who, despite her squalid surroundings, takes meticu-*
> *lous pride in her fried chicken. Both are attracted to each*
> *other's anachronistic temperament, and passion for finding*
> *beauty in ordinary things. Here, Clark confesses his love to*
> *Sylvia and asks her to run away with him to a place where*
> *they might both belong.*

CLARK: You and I don't belong up here, Sylvia. Life on the Turnpike
is fast, cheap, convenient, and dirty. Everyone's in a rush. And
what for? If you ask me, most of the miseries in the world are
caused by rushing — and when they're done rushing, nobody
ever knows what they were rushing to. That's why I have to
leave. I'm going where slow is still a value. Where people still
don't have anything better to do than savor a good meal made
with time and care.

[SYLVIA: *(Tentative.) And you want me to go with you?]*

CLARK: *(Embracing her.)* Yes! Think of it, Sylvia. You, me, and our
own fried-chicken restaurant. We'll change the way people look
at lunch. No more Value Express Meals, no more stamped-out
regulation portions, no more drive-through heartburn and
heartache. Nothing but slow-cooked Dixie chicken with eleven
Southern spices, homemade buttermilk biscuits and fresh tar-
ragon butter, all cooked with genuine passion by someone who
knows how. You, Sylvia. Come with me tomorrow and make it
happen.

Hurricane Iris
By Justin Warner

Louis: a professional snowboarder, late twenties

Comic

> *Louis and his fiancée, Nell, have traveled to Florida to spend time with Nell's mother Iris, an obscene, possessive, manipulative monster who has faked a terminal illness to lure Nell back to her. While there, Louis falls under a magic spell — intended for Nell — that has made him fanatically devoted to Iris. Here, his devotion reaches its climax.*

LOUIS: Iris, will you marry me?

[*IRIS: You've got to be kidding.*]

LOUIS: Believe me, there's some part of me that thinks I ought to be kidding, but I'm deadly serious. I can't explain it. I feel like I must be out of my mind. But for the past week I've been trying to make you happy. And listening to you now . . . hearing your tragic story of heartbreak and betrayal, I know that this is the greatest gift I can give to you . . . to truly devote myself to you with all my heart and soul. To bring joy to your last days on earth. To live for you and you alone. No matter what.

(I know, I'm supposed to be engaged to your daughter.) But think of how thrilled she'll be when she hears the news! All she wanted was for the three of us to live happily as a family, right? And now we will! And she'll see you happy at last, in your final hours! And we'll still get to spend time together — excluding, of course, the intimate moments you and I will want to share. And I can still marry Nell after you pass away, as a tribute to you. It all works out! Everything is going to be absolutely perfect!

Aguinaldo: Mark Twain in Purgatory
By Elaine M. Hazzard

Lieutenant Gregorio Del Pilar: twenty to twenty-three, dashing, courageous and vivacious. Freedom fighter Del Pilar by the age of twenty-three will become a general and give his life in battle to bravely prevent the capture of Generalissimo and President Emilio Aguinaldo

Seriocomic

Del Pilar, upon the suggestion posed by diplomat and fellow insurrecto Felipe Agoncillo that upon their return home to resume the battle against the Spanish the people may have forgotten the earlier valor of their leader Emilio Aguinaldo, responds to this challenge.

DEL PILAR: Yes, people have a short memory, Felipe, but there are things they could never forget. Not all their lives. The sight of Aguinaldo as he jumps up on the ramparts! We'd run out of gunpowder. He calls out to the Spaniards to fire! And they would! They'd fire and we'd see the cannonballs coming and he just jumps down. Most of them were duds. Sometimes the shells land so close to him they splatter him with mud. The kids loved that. They'd laugh to see him covered with mud! The children would pick up the shells and exchange them for rice at the ordnance unit. We'd take out the firing pins. Pour out the gunpowder. Melt down the metal for bullets! The people will remember our Generalissimo. *(Mock anger.)* Not another word against him, villano. *(Unsheathes sword for playful duel.)* En guardia!

The Leash of the Rainbow's Meow
By Kevin M. Lottes

Billy Bones: young man in his early twenties

Dramatic

> *Billy Bones is a born-again Christian in an overcrowded prison about to be freed on good behavior. In order to be freed, he must retrieve all the necessary signatures from the prison officers. The last signature he needs is from the "in-the-closet" homosexual warden, Harlen, who has genuinely fallen in love with him. Avoiding signing Billy's release form, the warden attempts to persuade Billy into staying at the prison with him by telling him that the outside world is a prison; in the warden's view, true freedom is in the prison's isolationism.*

BILLY: No, no, no — *you* got it all wrong! *This* place is a prison, these shackles and chains around my ankles — not the world — 'cause there ain't no life in here! I can't move forward in here, only in my mind, and that just ain't good enough for me! There is life out there! Life! God's children! People walking around. People going to church. People going to the bar across the street from the church — Lord help them to the other side of the road! People going to work. People watching their TV's at night and cuddling up with their husbands and wives, *their husbands and wives*, doesn't that just sound good together? People doing good, people doing bad — every day — and then there are people prayin', Harlen! And they're all prayin' for me and you! Isn't that beautiful? The world is not a prison, but a garden, sprouting every day with God's goods and God's bads to give us a good to fix the bad so that we all have a journey to make because without a journey what else would we all do but sit around feeling sorry for ourselves when we could be — "out there" — praisin' the Lord, planting more seeds?! There are people just dying to live — *I'm* dying to live! I was like you at one time — lost, but because of God's forgiveness, I've been given a clean slate, and I'm gonna show you what kind of a journey a man like me can make. There are leaps and bounds to be made and I'm gonna make 'em! Yes, we're all people imprisoned, but we're all awaiting the Glory of God to cut through our shackles and chains and with *what* I ask, with *what*? *Love.* It's love that does it. It's that simple. So don't tell me I'm walkin' into another prison 'cause being part of society *is* a garden, where hope is growing, and by the grace of God I will learn to be a farmer again!

The Dead Deportee
By Dan O'Brien

Ethan: twenties

Comic

> *Ethan, a Ph.D. candidate in literature, describes the nature of his passion for Meg, another Ph.D. candidate (as opposed to his feelings for his wife). Ultimately, Ethan wants to run away with Meg. Meg is actually "Mug," Meg's brain-damaged, identical twin sister.*

ETHAN: — I told her, Meg, I told her about us. *(Quick beat.)* I don't know why I need to destroy her like this. But I do. — Why did I marry her in the first place? I was young. I was your age. But men mature late. I was mentally twelve. No, four. I was a mental pygmy. Can you understand that, Meg? And she took advantage of my stupidity. But I wanted her so badly. And I truly believed I couldn't face this monastic death march of academic life without a hale and hearty woman by my side. A proud, handsome, somewhat doughy woman like Liz. Her figure revolts me now . . . But the truth is I think I wanted to make things harder for myself. — Yes! To guarantee I'd fail. So I would feel compelled to escape. To fly away like a thin, long-winged bird. To alight upon a new perch. Someplace real like Maine. Or Sedona. It doesn't matter. Someplace where I can live a realler life. With a realler woman . . . *(He takes her in his arms.)* Like you: my sweet, simple Meg . . . *(He kisses her.)*

Goin' North
from *Trains*
By Barbara Lebow

John Desfontaines III: in his early twenties with a lame foot. Experiencing his first taste of freedom, his moods can swing quickly from paranoia to joy.

Dramatic

> *A private railroad car in 1895. John is traveling north from his home in Louisiana with Gabriel Desfontaines, a family retainer, born a slave, who has been father and mother to his sickly charge. Gabriel has a hidden agenda, which John vaguely suspects: getting off the train in New York leaving John to fend for himself. The train has just gotten under way.*

[GABRIEL: *You really are happy now, ain't you?*]

JOHN: Free, Gabe, free! Flyin' away from home. Flyin' away from Louisiana! And you can pack that cane away. It only calls attention. I don't need it anymore. *(Suddenly afraid.)* Unless this is all a lie. A trick. *(Pause.)* The summer I was seven years old, remember? Suddenly there was a Christmas tree and presents and Granddaddy sayin' Father Christmas just came early this year and you keepin' your mouth shut and me knowin' it was because I was goin' to die before Christmas and everyone was lyin' to me. Is that what's goin' on now? You know something I don't, Gabe? Is that why they finally let me go? *(Pause, lifting out of the mood.)* I'm stronger than ever, Gabe! Three months! Three whole months doin' what I please without Granddaddy disapprovin'. I swear I'm goin' to — I'm goin' to go without my hat! I'm goin' to walk on the street like anyone else, chase women, talk to Yankees, cuss like a sailor, spit on the floor, fart — in public! Now don't start defendin' 'em, Gabe. I'll live to be ninety. My father doesn't really care and Granddaddy just thrives on his apprehension. You know what I'm talkin' about. It goes for you, too. Kick up your heels for a change. Let some of that stuffin' out of your shirt. This trip is supposed to be a present. Every minute that goes by, the train is carryin' us away from my sickly days and away from my schoolin' days and I don't want you teachin' me manners and cluckin' like a mother hen over everything I do. Maybe we'll like it so much up north, we won't come back. Either of us. Wine, women, and song, Gabe. Wine, women, and song.

Wilderness of Mirrors
By Charles Evered

James: early twenties

Dramatic

James explains what it is he likes about fishing, and in doing so, reveals why he would make a perfect spy.

JAMES: What is it I like about fishing? The waiting mostly. All the work you put into it and then the waiting. I'm partial to fly fishing, mostly. I went for the first time down in West Virginia with my father the summer before he died. He's the one who taught me all the differences and variations between the flies you tie, the colors you use, the shape of things. I love tying them on. Thinking what tiny, almost imperceptible little piece of it might just glimmer or gleam a little — what part of it I'm constructing might catch their eye. And I'll walk — up and down the riverbank having a look at all the different kinds of insects there, all the different species of things all along the ground. Just studying them. Because I know if I replicate that sort of creature exactly, tie it onto my hook, the fish in that particular area will be all the more familiar with it. All the more trusting of it. And so the "catch" for me begins hours — sometimes even days before my line ever hits the water. To tell you the truth, the fish on the end of my hook is more of just an afterthought, really. It's the waiting for me, that's the fun of it.

Eating for Two
By Barbara Lhota and Janet B. Milstein

Hal: early twenties

Comic

> *Hal has been talking to Nicole, twenty-six, online for the last few weeks. They've been spending hours and hours in private chat rooms and sending E-mails to each other. In the past week, they have begun talking on the phone. Today, they discuss plans to meet face-to-face.*

HAL: *(To audience, miming driving.)* God, I just keep sweating and sweating. Thank God I have my leather jacket. I won't take it off when I get to Denny's. If I ever find Denny's. It's so cool that she picked a breakfast food place for our first meeting. Most women choose overpriced bars with silly names like — Neo or Anti. Oh, I have met women before. Only eighteen or so times, but I didn't feel I was lying because it's never worked out. Besides, it's different with Superwoman. We are simpatico. After hours of amazing conversations, from existentialism to steakburgers, I'm finally going to meet her. Nicole's incredibly intelligent, has a great sense of humor, has her life together. I'm really thinking this may be the one! *(Beat.)* I think I'll play it cool though. I mean, she could be a lot uglier than her picture. Right?

Jugger's Rain
By Ron Mark

Jugger: twenty-two; innocent simplicity; plain, good face; small but strong; sensitive; protective; trace of a (dirt-poor) rural West Virginia accent

Dramatic

Jugger has buried his papa in the yard, to keep a promise that Papa would always be near Mama and Jugger's siblings. Mama doesn't know this, and overnight a tree grows on the secret grave. How Mama's unhappiness and terror change to mystical radiance, beauty, and joyous fulfillment, is told to older brother Carney (and Carney's wife Dulcy), by Jugger at the arcane tree. Jugger reveals, not only what he and Mama saw, but his own love and devotion for her.

JUGGER: That night after I buried Papa, I heard Mama scream. I run out here. She was standing right there, crying and pointing like this. That small tree, it had made . . . there was . . . a . . . Blossom. Just one. One perfect white blossom . . . It opened its tiny white fingers to Mama like this. *(Jugger opens his hand.)* And inside its fingers, way down deep was this one drop. It was just a rain drop only it has these colors coming out of it . . . A thousand colors like a diamond dancing in the sun. Only there wasn't any sun . . . Mama got so scared, so crazy, she just put out her hand like this, like at the altar, waiting for the ring. And that white flower, it bent down to kiss her hand. Then all its white fingers, they opened up. *(Palm turns upward slowly as if to receive a petal, but they drift down.)* The petals come off, floated down to Mama's feet like snow. And then she saw it. That little diamond drop, it just rolled out into the middle of her palm, right here . . . Papa always wanted to buy Mama a ring, but she wouldn't let him.

An Actor Prepares
By Mark Young

Trent: twenties, a young successful film actor

Seriocomic

> Trent asks his old boss out to breakfast one morning. They
> had a tempestuous, even violent, relationship when he was
> her office assistant and she is suspicious of his motives. At
> the time he worked for her he was a struggling actor and
> now he is one of the hottest young film stars in the country.
> He eventually tells her what he wants.

TRENT: I told you, I want my old job back. *(Beat.)* Oh *Sandy* No no
no . . . it's just for a few weeks. It's research. For the new
movie . . .? *P.A.* It's sort of a modernized *How To Succeed in
Business Without Really Trying* for the temp generation. We
start shooting in a few weeks and I just thought it would be useful to enter that . . . *place* again. Not to mention the article. *Van-
ity Fair* — they're thinking about me for the cover story. Right
before the movie comes out. They'd spend a week trailing us. It
would be a great story. The two of us. Our relationship. We
could relive that. After all, we were alike in a lot of ways. Both
intensely unhappy. Both going through hard times. You doing
anything, *anything* to hold onto your job in the dog-eat-dog
business world even as you plotted your climb up the few
remaining rungs of the corporate ladder. Taking it all out on me.
Me frustrated at having to work my menial day job, slaving
away as someone's assistant when I was really an artist made for
better things. Taking it all out on you. The two of us caught in
this death grip of . . . what . . . ? Dependence. Even as the finan-
cial gap between us widened every day. But amidst it all: my
humiliations, your tantrums and rages, the mind numbingly boring days . . . I always appreciated the opportunity to see how the
system works. From the bottom, you know? Ah, but since those
hellish times, I've managed to obtain some, shall we say, "philosophical distance." And what I've come to realize now that I'm

in a more *active* role is that it's easy to criticize when you're on the bottom. When you're not acting but just watching and dreaming. Of course it helps that I have my own personal assistant now . . . Yes, some hard times. But fun. So what do you say?

Donut Holes in Orbit
By Prince Gomolvilas

Joey: twenty-four

Dramatic

> *Joey's best friend, Alice, is leaving the country to go to college. He has admitted to her that he is in love with her. But that love is unrequited. It's strictly platonic. Here, he's saying good-bye.*

JOEY: Alice. I wanted to say, um, that you've . . . uh . . . been a really important part of my life, you know. I don't know if you know that or believe it, but it's true. I mean, I've lived in Modesto all my life, and I'm pretty much gonna die here, and everything here's so . . . the *same,* you know what I'm saying? I always know what's gonna happen every day, and it can be pretty boring. *(Pause.)* But out of all those predictable things that I can expect to see every day, I . . . always look forward to seeing you. I really do. *(Pause.)* And I understand what we talked about, and I understand how you feel and everything, and I just want you to know that I don't hold it against you or anything, and I don't know, I'm rambling, and I guess this is just my way of saying that I'm really gonna miss you. Alice. I'm gonna miss you a lot.

Jugger's Rain
By Ron Mark

Jugger: twenty-two; innocent simplicity; plain, good face; small but strong; sensitive; protective; trace of (dirt-poor) rural West Virginia accent

Dramatic

The vivid, searing, emotional images of the day and night their papa was killed — and the astonishing promise Jugger made and kept — are told to older brother Carney (and Carney's wife Dulcy), when Carney threatens him.

JUGGER: The day Papa died — day he burned up in the mine, laying on the ground — he pulled me down next to his face, his mouth all full of blood and smoke . . . The rain coming down on his face . . . His face all black with it . . . He *told me!!* . . . I swore *I'd do it* . . . I give my word that . . . I'd dig him up, the first night he was in the ground. You run off that night, Carney. Never come back. So I done it myself. It was his last words. I dug down with my shovel. Wasn't hard. Dirt wasn't even settled yet. I brung the hunting knife you gave me. Remember, Carney? . . . And got the casket open . . . First thing I saw was Daddy's face. The moon, it was looking over this shoulder here. Papa's face was different. Peaceful. Like the burns was all healed up, cooled off . . . I know it was crazy, but I started talking to him. I said, here I am, Papa, like I said I'd do. I took hold of his arms. He kind of smiled when I lifted him up, 'cept I know he didn't smile. And this sound came out of him, too. Kind of a . . . sigh. Yeah, a sigh like he was satisfied. Sound he'd make eating Mama's apple pancakes. *(Fighting the tears.)* He wasn't even cold. I took him down the hill on my back. He wanted to be with Mama, Isbel, everybody. *(Slowly.)* Then I done what I promised . . . I buried him again . . . *(Softly.)* Right here. *(Indicates tree and ground.)*

Grieving Space
By Barbara Lhota and Janet B. Milstein

Andy: late twenties

Dramatic

Kim and Andy's four-year-old daughter was kidnapped from her bedroom while they were making love one night.

ANDY: Please, Kim, don't push me away. I miss her like you cannot believe. Some nights I just wish we could hold each other and cry together instead of separately. *(Kim listens.)* I keep seeing so many days in my head. When you first told me that we were pregnant. At the hospital when I watched you give birth. Her first crawl and step and the way she held up her spoon in a triumphant, "I'm done!" But there's one night in my head that keeps coming back to me. I don't know why. It's so strange how smells and sounds come to your mind first. I think Isabella was about one and a half or so. It was fall. I remember it was fall right before Halloween. Because some of the neighbors were burning leaves. I like that smell. Poor little Bella cried all night because she had that terrible, miserable cold. She couldn't breathe — all stuffed up. *(Beat.)* She couldn't breathe. And you'd just about had it. You were so tired. Nothing had worked. She was fighting taking her medicine, and she just wouldn't stop crying all day. Not even Boo Boo could make her feel better. But I told you I'd stay up with her. And you fell asleep on the couch almost immediately. God, I'm so grateful for that night. I talked to her and played with her and cooed at her and rocked her. Finally, in the morning, right before dawn, she fell asleep. I was still holding her when you woke up. She looked so peaceful. I felt really good. Like I had done something. You put your feet on my lap. We didn't say anything at first. You just smiled at me and kissed me. Your face was so warm. Both of us were looking at Isabella. And you said, you said — *(Quietly.)* "You're a wonderful father."

Running Funny
By Charles Evered

Michael, early twenties, a sensitive young man just out of college

Dramatic

> *Michael explains to his friend from college how he tried to go back in time.*

MICHAEL: I tried to go back in time the other night. I did, really. I was at my sister's, and it was raining and windy and all that, but I didn't care. I just put on my jacket and walked right outside and walked straight in the direction of the house I used to live in with my parents. I started making myself believe that my parents would be there when I got there, ya know? Like all the time I've lived after they died has all been a dream or something, or some kind of TV show where you wake up one day and all of it was one long nightmare. And the closer I got to the house the more clearly I could see a light on in my mother's old room and I made myself believe that she had turned it on. And the closer I got the faster I wanted to get there until I was running, and I was crying too because I knew it was all make-believe I had made up inside my head and I knew that any minute now I would have to stop running and go back to where I really was. And I didn't want to. The last thing I feel compelled to do is go back to "real life." I don't see any point in it, really. I don't see any great advantage to "reality."

San Francisco Scarecrows
By Kevin M. Lottes

Ozzie Edwards: a young man in his early twenties

Dramatic

> *Ozzie Edwards and his best friend have traveled the countryside in search of Ozzie's long, lost father. An anonymous tipster tells them that his father was last spotted at a nearby bar in downtown San Francisco. As his best friend awaits Ozzie's return, Ozzie enters their hotel room having seen his father at the bar.*

OZZIE EDWARDS: He didn't even recognize me. Almost instantly, like a gunshot, I recognized him. At first, I couldn't move. I just stood there and watched him; he was by himself, drinking in a far corner booth. The place was packed. He was playing solitaire at his table. I stood there like a deer in headlights, trying to figure out my next move. I pulled my wallet out, to the picture of him that my mother had given me, to check it twice for good measure, but it didn't matter. I knew it was him. I was certain of it. A stream of smoke blew over his shoulders. I could hear the snap from each card as he slapped them down on the table. The whole place smelled like Cuban cigars, cheap lipstick, and bar stool leather. Everybody was making a ruckus: Shot glasses slammed down, Zippo lighters clicked, cowboy boots scuffed across the hardwood floor, outrageous women giggled, kissed, and hugged all kinds of backwards men; but not him, not me. When I finally built up enough courage to approach him, I moved to him with wide-open arms, I mean they were *wide* open, my arms, but he pretended like he didn't even know who I was. His own son. But I knew better than that. I felt it in his eyes. I was familiar to him. I could feel it move within him, right in the back of his eyes, where truth hits the hardest. But it didn't matter. We ended up going out the backdoor together, but we went down opposite sides of the street like two separate winds blowing under two separate skies. As if we were disconnected individuals, complete strangers, without a care in the world. How could he even act like that? He could've at least said "hey." Even if he said it as if it were some ancient-year-old obligation. I give up. I'm all worn out. It's time for me to find a new hero.

Leave
By Matthew A. Everett

Nicholas: a slightly rumpled man in his late twenties, works as a librarian at Indiana State University

Dramatic

> *Nicholas is speaking to his lover Seth, trying to make amends for an argument they had the night before. Seth, a Marine, came home on a brief leave because Nicholas' father had just died. The distance and secrecy necessitated by Seth's career and the military's "Don't ask, don't tell" policy have left Nicholas feeling alone and scared. Having Seth in the same room, nearby, overnight, has made a difference for both of them.*

NICHOLAS: I just wanted you to know — last night, with you here — that's the first decent night's sleep I've had in a long time, too. Definitely since my dad — *(He can't say the word* died.*)* He was just old, Seth. We all get old, eventually. I think he was just tired. My mom's been gone a while — there was never anyone else for him. That's a long time to be alone — walking the stairs at night. *(Pause.)* Ever since the morning I — found him — I haven't been able to sleep, not clear through the night. I always wake up — in the dark. And I lay there, wondering if that's what it was like for him. Waking suddenly for no reason, and realizing "This is it." But you know, at least he had something to look forward to. Either it was all over finally, or my mom would be there waiting. But I wake up — I can't do this alone. I'm not strong enough. I need you near me in the dark. So I can feel safe again.

Bring Back Peter Paul Rubens
By Barbara Lhota and Janet B. Milstein

Jerry: late twenties

Dramatic

> *Marlene has just accused her husband, Jerry, of being embarrassed about her weight and how people will perceive him because of it. Here Jerry explains to his wife the difficulties he had growing up and being overweight. He tries to help her understand why he's, at times, judgmental and insecure about how others judge both of them for being heavy.*

JERRY: No, I'm not. It's just . . . OK . . . when my father died, I started gaining weight. I mean, right when he died. Everybody and their brother kept bringing all this food to us. It's what people do. I don't know why. It's not like food would make up for my dad being gone. My dad was dead, but we had pies and cakes falling off our counters. I was always real confident before that too. My mother didn't want to talk about my father's death. Every time I brought it up, she'd invite me to sit down and eat. It was like it was supposed to make me feel better or something. And it did in the moment — until afterwards. It was kind of an obsession. Like keeping me connected to my dad. Before I knew it, I had put on fifty pounds. I couldn't believe it. I'd suddenly become . . . fat. I was dating this girl, Samantha, at the time. We were in gym class one day. We had one of those stupid rope things. I couldn't get up at all. I just kept slipping. My hands were all raw and burnt. And I was sweating like crazy. That never happened before. I was always pretty good in gym. And then these guys started laughing at me. Then they started cracking jokes about how fat I was. One of them turned to Samantha and oinked. He just kept oinking over and over. "It must be fun doing it with a pig! I'm amazed he hasn't squashed you yet." And then they all burst out laughing. Samantha broke up with me that very same day. She couldn't even look me in the face.

The Tangerine Quandary
By Diane Lefer

Theo Carlisle: twenties, a writer

Dramatic

> *Theo is trying to explain himself and gain sympathy from Liza who is outraged by the religious claims in the book he recently published.*

THEO: Liza, have you never lost someone? *(Beat.)* When my father died, I was at school. No one had even told me he was ill. He'd been buried before I knew. And I went to my classes and went to my room and walked around going through the same daily routine, wearing the same clothes, looking indistinguishable from the Theo of the day before. A person passing me on the street could not have known — Ah, his father just died! You know, my father and I were never close. But when he was gone — he was my origin, and without him, it's as though my existence was thrown into doubt. I'd be sitting on a chair or walking down a street, and suddenly feel myself plunging through empty space, spinning in the vacuum. Lost in the absence between atoms. I was bereft not just of a parent, but of all foundation, and when that's gone — But then I started to get these ideas! I realized I had no way of knowing what was carried in the hearts of the people I passed. Anyone of them might carry some terrible secret grief. They all looked so fragile to me, like little bits of vivified matter trying to stand their ground against the void. It made me treat people more gently — for a while. And then . . . I thought for the first time, what if someone among us carries not pain but a secret hidden glory? What if we must treat each and every person as if he or she is the One? I don't believe in God, you see, but I'm not sure I can bear to live in a world without one.

Here and There
By Adam Simon

Dan: early twenties, eager yet unsure

Dramatic

> *Dan's cousin killed himself five years ago. While at his cousin's house for the first time since the suicide, he happens upon a stack of pictures. He leaves the house immediately without a word to anyone. In the previous moment Dan's girlfriend just asked him what went on when he saw the pictures, why he had to leave.*

DAN: Whenever I look at a picture of him I wonder if it's there. I can't help it. I see old pictures of my cousin during what we thought was the beginning of his life but was actually the end and I wonder if it's in him yet. I look into his eyes wondering what stage the self-hatred has reached. In each expression, each asymmetrical tilt of the eyebrows I search for the kernel that eventually led to his death. I know it won't help, but I always feel like if I can just find the picture where it started, if I can look into his eyes in one of those pictures and see it, see the thought first enter his mind then I'll understand. I'll understand him and what happened and then move on and, I don't know — drink a cup of coffee or run a marathon . . . something.

It used to be funny when people would ask us to describe him and we'd say "well he's kinda negative, like if he won the lottery he'd be like *(Downtrodden voice.)* 'well I still gotta pay taxes.' " And we'd laugh. Well, of course he was manic depressive. I realized later that my impression was giving words to a diagnosis that I didn't understand yet. The highs and the lows and the general sense of doom in his demeanor, Christ I was too young to know what it all meant. Sometimes I catch the look when I'm watching television. Kurt Cobain will rub his chin at the end of the song and look toward his shoes and I swear to God that I can see it in him. It's not the first time he's thought about it, but it's — there are hurdles, you probably have to convince yourself to do it a total of 100 times before you actually do it. And when he rubs his chin, I think we see number ninety. It might not be that far, but it's serious, you can tell.

Flung
By Lisa Dillman

Devon: twenty-two

Seriocomic

In this monologue Devon tries to connect with his future sister-in-law by telling the story of his father's death.

DEVON: You weren't there when your dad died, I know. But I was *with* my dad and . . . well, I just . . . you know. It was like I wanted him to be so much more . . . whatever . . . *noble,* I guess. Or to accept it anyhow. As if the guy was supposed to turn around and be *philosophical,* for cryin' out loud. For *my* sake. And talk to me about my life. I mean . . . he really did *not* want to *go.* He got a really raw deal and he knew it. I think he was pretty pissed off . . . at the rest of us — my family, *everybody* — because we were going to go on and have our lives and he wasn't. And I just sat there during those last few weeks . . . reading Elizabeth Kuebler-Ross, ya know, and . . . *judging* him, really . . . thinking how much easier *I'd* try to make it on *my* family if it was me . . . But when I think about it now, I . . . I don't know . . . I wouldn't wanna go either! Heck, man, they'd have to drag me kicking and screaming down that tunnel. And all my dead relatives waving me toward the white light, egging me on. Forget *that.*

Canvas County
By Kevin M. Lottes

Curby Akers: a young man in his early twenties

Dramatic

> *Curby Akers is determined to save his hometown before it is to be completely renovated into a large, corporate paint plant. All the town's people have moved out, but Curby believes if he stays put that his hometown will be spared. A Lumberjack who is trying to convince him to "move along" with the rest of the town's people approaches him.*

CURBY AKERS: *You* need to be "cut" out! How would *you* like it if I took a chain saw and cut *you* out so that I could build say a . . . paint plant . . . of all things — as if we need another one! We got plenty of *you*, why not cut *you* out to build something else that's just going to go bankrupt in ten years, be emptied out because the people operating it had eyes that were bigger than their stomachs? It's empty, empty, empty and there's not a hint of it anywhere that it's going to stop as long as there's people like *you* who need a paycheck to pay their bills, to put food on the table and a roof over their heads. It's about consumption is what it is; complete consumption until you get to the point where you don't even fully realize what you're actually consuming anymore because you've been brainwashed to only think about your *immediate* needs. I feel it now; I want it now; I will *take* it now! Why do we need another paint plant . . . another gas station, another restaurant, another *Wal-Mart* for cryin' out loud? No, it's madness is what it is! It's madness because it's *excess* — all completely unnecessary. It's out of control and it's pretty much *our* fault; it's *my* fault, and that's what's so damn frustrating about all this. The landscape is being demolished into one great big billboard that says, "Oh, yeah, we have one of those here too!" I'm so sick of it! All I want to do is save this one little patch of grass. That's it, that's all I want to do. Because when I see one little blade of grass, surrounded by a bed of concrete, trying to break its way out, I feel like there's still some hope. Now . . . is that too much to ask for?

The Imperious Aunt
By John McGarvie

Julian Laird: twenty-four, third year law student, angry, distrustful, a loner.

Dramatic

> *The title represents one of the main characters, the Baroness Margaret Vinegar, an outspoken woman in her mid-seventies who is Julian's aunt. A widow, she has returned to New York from Britain and is invited by Philip, Julian's father, to stay in their apartment. The two men themselves have a distant relationship; Julian's mother died when he was eight; he has never forgiven her. The domineering Baroness takes over their home; she even redecorates. Julian resents her; he fears her; she is a direct link to his mother; her presence awakens the pain he has successfully buried. The Baroness demands that he call her Aunt Margaret and stop using her title when addressing her. That demand gives him the opportunity to rail against her, as we see in this monologue.*

JULIAN: Look, Baroness . . . I mean, Aunt . . . look.
(Rises off the sofa to face her.)
    You stormed into this apartment so fast . . . the Pentagon could learn from your lightning strike maneuvers. You barged into our lives without a care for who we are, or what our lives are all about. You start taking over. Changing the furniture. Painting the walls. Your secretary phones here, giving me orders. Telling me when I can and cannot be here. In my own home. You don't know me, and I don't know you. Until Dad mentioned you a few weeks back, I didn't even know you existed. I didn't know I had an aunt who lived in England. You never bothered to keep in touch. Now all of a sudden you care so much about us you need to move in. And you didn't exactly arrive as the motherly older aunt, with candies and cookies. That's not how you presented yourself to me. Why should I call you Aunt Margaret? You didn't earn it.

(Pauses. He stares at her. She's looking away, her chin high.)

You showed up like a general, with your tank parked outside the door. It's your world now, and we should be grateful that you're giving us . . . allowing us . . . a peek inside.
(Pauses again.)

No way, lady. You came in here as the Baroness. That's what you are to me. That's how you'll leave. That's the way it has to stay.

You Been Lied To
By Barbara Lhota and Janet B. Milstein

Jack: young adult

Dramatic

> *Jack just found out from a stranger that the woman he thought was his sister his whole life was really his biological mother.*

JACK: You and her are so alike. You lie to me for years and then you expect me to accept your apology just like that. It doesn't matter at this point. *(Yells.)* So go away! Oh, I'm sorry. Worried about the neighbors? *(Opening the door a crack, yelling louder.)* The neighbors? The hell with the neighbors! We're talkin' about losing the basic pieces of who I am. Having everything all mixed up and put together in some twisted new story. You're worried about how the neighbors will look at you? Well, how have they looked at *me* all these years?! Ever think of that? *(Beat.)* You come home pregnant at thirteen. Next thing they know *Grandma's* changing my diaper, and I'm calling *you* sister. They must have been whispering like crazy all that time. Did everyone in this damn neighborhood know besides me? *(Beat.)* How thoughtful of you to come here and tell me that my entire life has been a lie. But what's there to talk about now? How can I talk to her or you? How am I ever supposed to believe either of you again?

Bats
By N. M. Brewka

Kevin: twenty

Dramatic

> *When Kevin's college baseball coach refuses to allow him to play with a broken collarbone for the pro scouts, Kevin explodes.*

KEVIN: How can you do this to me? Why the hell should I be a good sport? You can take your good-sport shit and — hey, I get it. You're pissed that I play better ball than you ever did. I'm right, aren't I? Every time I hit a homer, you must be pissed as hell. You're nothing but a friggin' control freak. You're a two-bit, lousy part-time coach at a fucking two-bit junior college and you think you're God. Well, the hell with you. I don't care what you think. Your coaching sucks and so do you. I quit.

Companion Piece
By David A. McElroy

Carl: late twenties, Jasmine's boyfriend. He works in a sporting
goods store and lives with his older sister. He thinks of himself
as "a man about town." He is an alcoholic, an abuser, and
believes he is put upon by women.

Dramatic

> Carl has just caused his girlfriend, Jasmine, to cry. He made
> her a vodka and tonic with limes and she is allergic to them.
> He tries to explain his side to Winona, Jasmine's friend that
> is over for the evening.

CARL: No! Let her get it out of her system. I've tried to talk to her
when she cries and she just won't listen. She's so damn sensitive!
If I say the wrong thing or horse around with her a little, she gets
all weepy on me. She's not tough. Seems like I'm always apolo-
gizing for one thing or another. She does piss me off sometimes.
I mean look at what just happened! She always drinks screw-
drivers. Always. She's never had a vodka and tonic in the whole
time I've known her. How the hell am I supposed to know that
she's allergic to limes for Christ sake!? I can't even remember if
she ever told me. We've only been goin' around together for a little while. It's not our chief topic of conversation. And another
thing. She doesn't like sports. Hell, I'm a sports fanatic! I work
in a Sporting Goods store, I go to the gym every day and work
out, I go to all the major league games in St. Louis; I love sports!
She thinks it's dumb. You know. I don't know a lot about you
women. You're so soft on the inside and hard on the outside. I
try not to ask too much. I try to be understanding, but God I
make a little mistake and all I get back is crap! It's amazing!

Back to School
By Barbara Lhota and Janet B. Milstein

Greg: late twenties

Comic

> *Greg and Tess have been living together for several years.*
> *Tess has gotten into the habit of spending large sums of*
> *money at Office World and other office-supply stores.*
> *Things have gotten worse than ever since Greg's hours at*
> *work have increased. Crisis point hit when they realized she*
> *had maxed out several credit cards. Greg has been under-*
> *standing and has even gone with Tess to Shopaholics Anony-*
> *mous meetings, but he has now reached his limit. Tonight,*
> *he has found some suspicious, new-looking paper products.*

GREG: Tess, you went to Office World unaccompanied, without
phoning for help first, and of your own free will — despite your
promises to me, Shopaholics Anonymous, and to yourself. *(Los-*
ing it.) How do you spend two hundred and seventy-four dollars
at an office supply store? *(Beat.)* I'm not excited! I'm broke!
(Reacting to her face.) OK. I think we should stop and have a
meeting right now. I know it's not Wednesday, but this is a spe-
cial meeting. It's a keep-a-roof-over-our-heads-until-Wednesday
meeting. Just the two of us. Of course all SAA rules will remain
intact so there is no cross talk. Now. Who wants to start? OK,
I will. No cross talk please. *(Takes a long deep breath.)* I put up
with the converting our living room into an office. I even bought
you the connecting file cabinets and the revolving computer
stand. Even though you don't have a home business. I know you
like to be organized but there has to be a limit. I have been going
to the Shopaholic meetings with you every Wednesday. I listen to
you. I support you. But now I want to kill you.

Heaven and Home
By Matthew A. Everett

Vincent: male, late twenties to early thirties, works at a video rental store

Dramatic

> *Vincent is lashing out at his younger brother Cian, who insists that their late friend Byron's ghost is haunting him. Byron was Vincent's best friend, despite the fact that Byron was gay and Vincent straight. When Cian came out as a young gay man, Cian and Byron had something in common that made Vincent feel left out. Despite harboring a crush on Byron, Cian could hardly bring himself to visit the hospital when Byron was dying. Vincent was a constant presence at Byron's bedside till the end. But once again, a connection with his best friend is eluding him, and coming easily to his brother.*

VINCENT: I admit it's weird to be fighting for custody of a ghost but I don't care! He should *not* be haunting you. You're my little brother. I knew him first. I knew him longer. I was at the hospital every day. You visited once. But he comes to you?! He haunts you? He visits you? Talks to you? How do you think that makes me feel?! He was my best friend. *My* best friend. To you, he was — what? — someone convenient to be hung up on so you didn't have to go out and develop any real personal life, take any real chances? Fellow member of your little homosexual sorority? I mean, look at you! Dead two years, he wasn't even your boyfriend, and here you are still playing the widow, haven't even so much as gone out on a date!

I don't care that it's probably all in your head! If you're nuts, you're lucky! I'd give anything to be that kind of crazy. 'Cause you see, I don't have that. No visits. No talks. No friendly ghost. All I've got is past tense. And that shit fades so fast. There's this huge chunk of my life now that's gone completely out of focus. Before, if I got lost or confused or off track, all I'd have to do is talk to him, not even about the problem, just talk about anything, because he understood me. He was everything I'd lived through. Now I don't know what the fuck I'm doing anymore! And he comes to you.

Leave
By Matthew A. Everett

Nicholas: a slightly rumpled man in his late twenties, works as a librarian at Indiana State University

Dramatic

> *Nicholas is arguing with his lover Seth, a Marine stationed overseas who is home for a brief leave due to the death of Nicholas' father. Despite the strains that living under the secrecy of the military's "Don't ask, don't tell" policy have put on their relationship, Seth wants to continue to have a career in the Marines and has asked Nicholas to leave the only home he's ever known and follow him.*

NICHOLAS: Say I leave here? What am I doing it for? For you? What about us, Seth? What is this doing for us? I get out from under my parents' roof, I leave Terre Haute and follow you — for what? We still can't be open. If you stay in the Marines, nothing changes! Seth, you brought me out. You're the reason I know who I am. I can't go back, not even for you. If you're just putting on a uniform for my dad's sake, he's dead! You can stop trying to impress him! And you don't have to impress me. You pulled my heart out of my chest and showed it to me, and I lived. Even if you walk out of my life tomorrow — and God, I hope that's not what we're talking about here but even if you did — you have marked me for life. I can't be unselfish where you're concerned. I need you with me! As long as you're a Marine, I can't visit you. I can't see you. I can't touch you. I can't hold you. I can't even write you! All I have, all that's real, are the couple of times a year you manage to get away from the military. And come back here. Occasional visits. That's not a real relationship, it's a distant cousin! The kind of cousin you only see at christenings, weddings, and funerals. Well, guess what?! I ain't having kids, this country won't let us get married and I'm fresh out of parents to bury for you!

The Face of God
By Justin Warner

Brad: a harried young angel filling in for God, twenty to thirty

Comic

> *God, it seems, has taken a leave of absence leaving Brad in*
> *charge of his many duties. Here, overworked Brad unloads*
> *on a new arrival to the celestial kingdom.*

BRAD: Yes! Acting God! That's my title, OK? I'm performing the
duties of the Almighty with His full authority until that time that
He returns!

[GRENDEL: *Which is when exactly?*]

BRAD: I don't know! The bastard just walked out! I've been stuck
here taking care of his crap for sixteen years! And there's no
vacation, Mr. Grendel. No golf weekends. Not even a bathroom
break. If you leave your heavenly post for even a second your
soul gets destroyed! That's policy.

[GRENDEL: *(Interested.) You don't say.*]

BRAD: Oh, you don't know the half of it, pal. We've got poultry plant
working conditions up here. Sure, we all take these jobs because
we need the redemption, but let me tell you, Mr. Don't Take My
Name in Vain rides that for all it's worth! I mean, even before he
took off, he never really *did* anything. Just sat around, passed
judgment, and read *The Economist*. And one day, I'm in here
doing some filing, and the G-man says to me, "Brad, I'm going
for coffee — could you mind the desk while I'm gone?" I said
sure. That was the last I ever saw him! "I'm going for coffee."
What the hell was that? I mean, he could just *zap*, make the coffee right there, right? How could I let him screw me over like
that? If I ever see him again, I swear I'll kick his lazy omnipotent
ass from here to Cleveland!

Celestial Motions
By Mrinalini Kamath

Jake: Caucasian male, age twenty-five

Seriocomic

Jake has been roommates for the past six months with Leela, an Indo-American woman. They have been friends since they were in college together. The only reason Leela's parents have been OK with this arrangement is because she had convinced them that Jake was gay (something that Leela herself was inclined to believe). A series of events causes Jake to realize that he has loved Leela as more than a friend ever since they were in college. He proclaims his love and Leela returns it. However, her parents are less than thrilled to find out that Leela is dating a non-Indian. Leela thinks that her parents might be reassured if Jake paid a visit to her parents' house. Jake does, and this monologue is what he says by way of introduction.

JAKE: Well, I just . . . heh, I was going to say that I just happened to be in the neighborhood, but that probably won't wash, will it? *(He laughs nervously.)* Uh, actually, I, um, I wanted to meet you — well, not really *meet* you, because we've met before, when you used to visit Leela at school, and . . . and . . . when she moved in, but that was uh, before we decided to uh, you know, get together. *(Pause, as if waiting for a response that doesn't come.)* So, I thought — I know that Leela said that you weren't entirely happy hearing about us being together now, and I'm sure . . . I'm sure it was a shock, what with you thinking I was gay and all, which, you know, I'm *not*. I've only dated girls, lots of . . . well, not lots, just a few, a couple, before I told Leela how I uh, how I feel. And, uh, speaking of how I feel, I just wanted to let you know that my uh, my intentions toward your daughter are completely honorable . . . and I respect her. A lot. And I'll never hurt her, or let her down. *(Pause.)* Yeah, that was . . . uh, I think that was what I wanted to say. Do you have any questions for me, about my background, or my . . . prospects?

Tapster
By N. M. Brewka

Brian: a male in his early twenties

Comic

> *Trying to earn money to finish up a long undergraduate college career, Brian applies for a job in a bar only to discover both its owner, Phil, and the clientele are all recipients of sex-change operations.*

BRIAN: You know, many times I've wanted to change things about myself, too. Like, I wish I could speak French, and my car, yeah, I'd definitely change my car. Not that I'm comparing dumping my grandma's Honda Civic to your, your, you know, body mechanics. And I wish I could finally get my degree without all the hassle of taking courses, but I guess it doesn't work that way. The one class I really liked was this mixology class, even though it was only half a credit. I mean, how cheap is that? It's like somebody leaving you a nickel tip. But, the good thing is, I think I may have found my niche. That's pronounced nitch, right? *(Beat.)* Oh, OK, it's like I said about the French thing. *(Draws it out.)* Neeshe.

Speechless
By Paul Kahn

Man: twenties, nervous-looking

Comic

A park on a sunny summer day. An attractive young woman sits on a bench, reading a book. A young man approaches and begins speaking to her. She appears not to hear him. But, at times she may frown, smile, run her fingers through her hair, or look up as though she is vaguely aware of some disturbance in the atmosphere around her.

MAN: Excuse me, I don't mean to disturb you, but . . . Well, obviously I do in a way. I mean it's obvious you're sitting there reading your book, enjoying the sun, perfectly content by yourself. But there's something I just have to tell you.

I've been watching you. Not staring. I haven't been staring. I swear to God I have not been hiding in the bushes like some kind of perverted stalker. But I couldn't help seeing that you're . . . And I don't mean this to sound like I'm coming on to you. Oh no, I swear to God I'm definitely not trying to come on to you. That doesn't mean you're not attractive. Or that I'm not . . . I mean I'm normal, absolutely normal, in the sense that I'm not abnormal, like, you know, I don't like little boys or . . . or sheep.

You probably get this all the time. You're probably sick of it. You're probably thinking: Another man, right, another superficial jerk, just fixated on what's on the outside and doesn't give a damn about what's inside you. Believe me, I'm not that way. I would absolutely love to get inside you!

I don't mean like that! Oh God, I'm making a mess of this! What I'm trying to say is I know you have a brain. Probably an absolutely stunning brain. But because of the way the sun is lighting up your yellow hair and your soft-looking cheek and other places I JUST CAN'T THINK ABOUT ANYTHING ELSE!

Atheist Comedy
By Ron Riekki

Willie: early twenties

Seriocomic

> *Willie explains his relationship with his girlfriend to his psychiatrist.*

WILLIE: Well, I'm unemployed still. And I haven't been getting along with my girlfriend. I mean, I *have*. I love her, and she loves me. A lot. That's obvious. But . . . I dunno . . . I . . . we . . . still haven't. . . you know. . .
(Tries to come up with a way to symbolize sex. Makes a circle with his thumb and forefinger and starts to poke through it with a finger from his other hand, but he feels uncomfortable with that. So he makes two fists and does a rocking motion, but this is only worse. Decides to stick with putting it into words.)
     We haven't constipated the relationship. And I was thinking that may be . . . something, that's been on my mind. A little. Bit. Often. Much. All the time. Having sex. Is on my mind, all the time . . . And she's slept around with like . . . twelve guys. That's almost a dozen. I don't get it. I'm a virgin and I'm male. I'm not supposed to be the virgin. She's supposed to be the virgin. She says this crap about wanting to make it special with me and not screw things up and she's a born-again virgin and I wonder why the line gets drawn with me. Being the nice guy sucks! I, I, it j-, it doesn't make sense.

Atheist Comedy
By Ron Riekki

Willie: early twenties

Comic

> *Willie's girlfriend thinks he might be gay, but Willie tries to explain that he's actually an atheist.*

WILLIE: No. No-no-no-no. No, no-no-no-no-no-no-no-no-no! No. No. I'm not gay. At least I don't think so. I mean, I do like Mandy Patinkin. But I've always masturbated to females, so I think that makes me heterosexual. In a sad and lonely way. Although a lot of pornography has lesbians, and lesbians are homosexual; so, therefore, I could be homosexual through osmosis. But . . . what I was trying to . . .
(Clears throat.)
    What I'm trying to tell you is that. . .
(Takes a deep breath.)
    Ummmmmmmmmmmmmmmmmm, you know how you're *really* into spirituality? And how you *really* believe in God? OK, um, I'm . . . I am . . . I'm really, *really* . . . an atheist.

You've Got To Be Sitting
By N. M. Brewka

Jason: late twenties to thirties, a portrait painter

Comic

Jason, a portrait painter, reacts when Tim, a potential customer in his twenties, starts pulling out nude photos of Jason's sister, Sheila, asking him to paint her from a photo as a surprise birthday present for her.

JASON: Tell me tell me, Tim, do you think it's right to be showing a total stranger this woman's picture? I mean, OK, I'm an artist, I paint portraits for a living, but for all you know I'm a total whack job. How do you know I won't stalk this woman? She's drop-dead gorgeous, right? So, if you're going to share such a beautiful woman with the universe, what if the universe strikes back? In my opinion, this girl, this woman, this complete and total stranger — let's call her Sheila, Tim, just for fun — oh, really? Her name is Sheila? Well, how about that. See, it's what I was just saying. Put her out there in the universe without her bloomers and the universe will do odd things. This isn't me talking, Tim. This is God. God, the universe, me, we all say Sheila should at least be wearing a thong.

Just Trying to Be Friendly
from *Conventional Behavior*
By G. L. Horton

Hal: late teens to early twenties, a nice but nerdy physics student, not an outstanding physical specimen

Seriocomic

> *Hal and the beautiful Queenly Character he is talking to are in the hallway of the hotel where Hal is attending his first Science Fiction Convention. He is wearing jeans and a Star Trek T-shirt and looking for kindred spirits — especially female ones.*

HAL: Great costume! Bet you win a prize. . . . Sorry. I didn't mean to stare. You're so beautiful I don't think I thought you were real. I — uh — I've never been to a Sci Fi Con before. — Oh, yeah, right. Don't call it Sci Fi. *(Abashed.)* I seem to keep putting my foot in it. I don't even know — I'm all tangled up. I feel so — weird. — Right! Maybe not weird enough! Not as weird as everybody else! That's what Ken told me: "In science fiction, weird is standard." Ken was supposed to bring me to this, but his uncle died. Anyway, Ken looks forward to the convention all year, you know? Cause women at Cons aren't like regular girls — I mean like — civilians? . . . "Mundanes" — right. Ken said we'd be able to — could talk to you — . Except I can't. Total strike-out. If I'd known I'd be on my own, I'd've had him rehearse me. The way Ken described it, all I'd have to do was walk into a party. I tried that. Last night. On the nineteenth floor. It took me forty minutes to get into an elevator: There were huge crowds and some people had figured it out so they could be in front exactly as the door opens? Shove in all their friends. When I finally got on, instead of going up, it goes to the basement and gets stuck there: Some techie's idea of a joke, I guess. But I got blamed for it! I never touched the buttons, honest! They were like a lynch mob! They threw me off, and I had to walk, subbasement to nineteen, twenty-one floors. I hadn't brought an ID, so I couldn't get a beer. Not that I'm that big on alcohol, but it might have helped. To deal with Elfs. Elves. It was decorated all like — like — And they were all standing around being — Them. They had big pointed ears and costumes — well, little bits of fur over lots of skin. Anyway, they all knew who they were. Each of them was somebody I was supposed to recognize, you know? After about six words they'd realize I didn't, and just walk away. Talk about alien!

Black & White
By Mark Young

Owen: eighteen to twenty, a sailor

Dramatic

> *Owen and Jasmine meet one night on an el platform. They*
> *are two people from opposite sides of the tracks. He is a*
> *sailor who grew up in Iowa. She is a worldly art student. He*
> *is on leave, seeing the city for the first time. He asks her out*
> *for a milkshake and she politely refuses, insisting she's not*
> *wholesome enough for a milkshake. It eventually becomes*
> *clear that she's refusing him and not the milkshake.*

OWEN: What's that supposed to mean? What? You don't like milk-
shakes? . . . I wasn't asking you to . . . I just . . . What I . . .
wholesome — I meant wholesome. *(Beat.) I* think you are. I
really think — . . . You were wholesome enough to give me
directions. *(Beat.)* I'm sorry. I'm dense sometimes. Spell it out.
(Beat.) I see. So it's not you. It's me. Because I'm in the Navy,
right? And because I'm from Iowa. A farm boy. Innocent . . . But
you've got it all wrong. My dad? You know those x-rated mag-
azine places you see off the side of the highway surrounded by
cornfields with pickups and semis in the parking lot? My dad
opened one of those when our farm started to go under. He cut
it right out of the cornfield. Now all of those trucks that used to
whiz by pull off the side of the road at our farm and we sell them
magazines and videotapes. I worked there before I enlisted. And
the Navy? The *cook,* the cook at the base . . . ? He sells heroin
on the side. And half of the guys in my unit? They're so out of
their minds . . . well, you don't even want to know. *(Beat.)* Look,
I'm telling you this because you were *nice.* You gave me directions. I know it's not much. I just thought . . . A date. What do
you say? I'm asking you for a date Jasmine.

Bats
By N. M. Brewka

Sam: male, twenty

Comic

Sam, mascot for the Fighting Felines junior college baseball team, is trying to ask the gorgeous and brainy Miranda out.

SAM: Oh, hi, Miranda. Say, I heard you aced the poli-sci final. Man, that is so cool. Do you want to be president or something? I mean, don't get me wrong, I think you'd make a fine First Lady, no, wait, I guess that's only if you married a guy who became president, which sure isn't me. Not that I'm not presidential material, mind you. I can name ten people right off the top of my head who'd like to shoot me. And by the look on your face, I can see I'd better make that eleven.

either/or
By Dan O'Brien

Eric: twenties to early thirties

Comic

Eric is giving career advice to a young actor in a coffee shop in New York City.

ERIC: I'm just trying to help you understand, Stefan. That's all. — Your name is Stefan, isn't it? I'm trying to give you some guidance, some sort of model. O sure, I was like you, *proud;* but that was before my one-man show became a hit off-off-off-Broadway. It's a performance piece centered around the idea of my penis. Maybe you've heard of it: "The Imperceptible Spatula," or "Hard On!," and the thematic content has to do with postmodern man coming to grips with his genito-urinary tract. With heady material like that you need some comic relief. So my dick, in homage to a good friend of mine — another performer who really came up with the idea anyway and yet I don't credit him I don't know why I'm such a bastard in a mysterious yet daring sort of way — my penis performs impersonations of dead English royalty. Richard II, for example, in which I sling my testicles up over my penis like a hunchback. Or Henry VIII, where I outfit my penis with a very small drumstick, but not too small because I'm very well endowed. Have I mentioned my endowment? I never have to work another day as long as I live. But I work out four days a week. So I guess my next question for you is this: What are you willing to do to get where you want to go?

Vent
By Sean Patrick Doyle

Jeff: male, mid-twenties

Comic

> *A flamboyant young actor, who longs for leading roles in works by the greats, practices Euripedes in the bathroom. He thinks he is insufferably effeminate and attempts to butch it up while practicing for his newest television spot, a Hot Pockets commercial.*

JEFF: *Zeus, thou hast heard her? Thus I am cruelly*
Spurned and derided by this ravenous
Lioness, this murderess of children!
Yet, fiend, in thy spite for the dead will I raise
a lamenting dirge, loudly invoking
Heaven to be witness, how thou hast —

Taken four fucking years of acting training, and it's toilet bowl productions presents *Medea*. You are the only person who sees this. *(Points at the mirror image.)* You. *(Looks and finds something between his cuspid and one of his front teeth. He picks at it.)*

But everyone gets to see Hot Pockets, Jeff. Hot Pockets. Mmm. *(Thinks.)* Hmmm. *(In a different manner.)* Mmm. *(Different manner.)* Mmmmm. Hot Pockets. Mmmmm. Crispy, crusty, tender, fl — faggot. You sound like a faggot, Jeff. You are a faggot. But not on TV. You are the regular Joe who played basketball in high school! Throw me the ball. *(Lowering voice.)* I'm open. Pass me the ball. I am Joe, the average American college student who loves his Hot Pockets.

Mmmmm. Mmmmmmmm. Hot Pockets. Crispy, crusty. *(Stops. Less flamboyant.)* Crispy, crusty, tender. Fuck. *(Pause.)* Where's the Mamet?! Hot Pockets? You can't even do Hot Pockets. You faggot. *(Butch.)* You faggot. *(Silence. Focuses, then.)* Crispy, crust, tender, flaky, crust. Mmmm. I love *(Corrects himself.)* I love my Hot Pockets. *(Smiles, holding his imaginary Hot Pocket.)* Here I come. Mmmm. *(Large, Cheshire cat grin. Exits.)*

Quiet Misty Meadows
By Barbara Lhota and Janet B. Milstein

Bart: twenties, a mourning, pet-cemetery patron

Comic

> Bart has come to Quiet Misty Meadows Cemetery to make
> arrangements for his recently deceased pet fish, Moo Moo.
> Annette, thirties, the director of Quiet Misty, has just had all
> four wisdom teeth removed and has taken some heavy-duty
> medication to try to ease the pain. As the scene begins,
> Annette is beginning to explain the ceremonial options to
> Bart.

BART: Would we be able to view her before we take her to her final
resting place? I would love to have an open casket, but she's so
disfigured and *(Tearful.)* it's all my fault. I let my stupid brother
watch her and he has cats. I told him to keep her away from
them, I told him, but those nasty little beasts pulled her out of
the tank and started to — it's my fault that she's, that she's . . . I
know, I know I *shouldn't* . . . *(Realizing.)* What did you say? You
look like you want to laugh. *(She shakes her head no.)* Well, I'm
having second thoughts about the burial. I don't think it's natural for her. And your suggestion that we sink her is sick. I think
it's sick! I think you're sick!! I think this whole place is sick!!!
She was exotic!! *(Angry.)* Can't you understand?! You evil witch!
(Breaks down in tears.) It was terrible to die like that. Those
cruel monsters tore her from my bosom. And now I have to live
and go on without her. I have to return home to her things. To
her little treasure chest and her little snorkel guy and her little
seahorsey and . . . her little . . . net. I loved her, Ms. Hope. We
had a connection. And every time I walk past her fish flakes, I
think of us. She won't nibble or moo moo anymore! Do you
understand that? And the question remains, what will I do with
all the little pebbles at the bottom of the tank? I can't just throw
them out. What will I do with them?

Will You Please Shut Up?
By Dan O'Brien

Tom: late twenties to early thirties

Comic

> *Tom and Sylvia have not seen each other since their break-*
> *up a few years ago; till one day they sit next to each other*
> *on the subway. Quickly they're back to their old routines,*
> *their intense love-hate dynamic. Here Tom is trying to catch*
> *Sylvia up on the surprising turn his life has taken.*

TOM: WILL YOU PLEASE GOD PLEASE JUST STOP IT PLEASE?
(Beat.)
Three minutes and it's already back to the same old horror. You
know what? I'm so glad we ran into each other today, because
now I know — I know we did the right thing in breaking up.
God, why can't you leave me alone?! I'm an adult now, Syl! Not
a kid anymore, Syl! I've cured my chronic hives. I've been to Hell
and back again, and I've learned a lot about my Self! And if I
need to stand up on stage in fishnet hose and three-inch heels
and belt out Bette Midler tunes just to feel like a "whole person," then that's "OK." OK? It's better than OK — it's fabulous!
And you know why? Because I love it! Syl: Do you have any idea
what it feels like to put on foundation, and "falsies," and "sexy"
underwear and the finer points like mascara, eyeliner, lipstick,
the wig. — The wig, Syl! O, how I love that gorgeous wig! It's
blonde and Germanic and when I step out on stage . . . I know
I'm beautiful.
(Beat. A subway stop; people get off and come on.)
[SYLVIA: *Are you gay, Tom?*]
TOM: No I'm not gay.
[SYLVIA: *Because I always thought you were. A little — "gay."*]
TOM: Why does everybody just *assume* all drag queens are gay?

Sniff Sniff, Ahh Ahh
By Barbara Lhota and Janet B. Milstein

Aaron: late twenties, a young creative writer for an advertising firm

Comic

> *Aaron heads up a team in the creative area at an advertising firm. He and Kim have been working all night to satisfy their client. Currently, he is working on the new Inhalo nasal spray campaign. Kim is the Inhalo account manager. Kim is listening intently to Aaron as he desperately tries to brainstorm ideas.*

AARON: I came up with the idea a week ago. I can see it now. It's part of the jungle theme. *(Acting it out.)* It's all misty and hot. Misty, misty, hhhot, hhhot. The grumpy, sniffily gorilla with the stuffed-up nose growls *(Growls.)* at the poor chirping birds. *(Chirps.)* You be the birds, Kimmie. *(She has no idea what this entails.)* He scares them. *(Growls at Kim who jumps a bit, trying to be a bird.)* Then ta-da! He spies the Inhalo Nasal Spray among the coconuts. Curious, he smells the bottle and his strong hand squeezes it — *(He looks at her.)* OK, paws, whatever. I'm on a journey here. And then he inhales *(Inhales.)* Ahh. It is good. He sniffs again. Ahhhh, he can breathe again. Suddenly, he becomes this gorgeous tan Tarzan with bulging muscles. The birds gather round him, singing, and a scantily clothed woman smiles from behind a palm tree. The music. The caption. "Inhalo — get back to your real nature." *(He relishes the moment.)* Huhn? Huhn? *(She's uninspired by it.)* Sure, shoot down my ideas, but can *you* think of anything? No! *You* come up with "a jungle theme" for nasal spray — oh, of course! But suddenly when I add a gorilla and Tarzan, it's all wrong!

Sniff Sniff, Ahh Ahh
By Barbara Lhota and Janet B. Milstein

Aaron: late twenties, a young creative writer for an advertising firm

Comic

> *Aaron heads up a team in the creative area. Currently, he is working on the new Inhalo nasal spray campaign. Kim is the Inhalo account manager. Aaron and Kim have both moved ahead quickly — Kim for her selling abilities, Aaron for his success on last year's "feel the rush" mint copy. Aaron and his team, unbeknownst to the very busy Kim, have been stuck on the nasal spray copy. Kim has come to look at preliminary workups the night before the presentation is due, only to find that there is no copy written.*

AARON: It's nasal spray, Kim. How much context do we need? The bottle says it's nasal. It says it's spray. People automatically intu-it that it's a bottle to sniff, to clear the nose. Will people think it's for their armpits? No. Will they mistake it for anti-anxiety medication? A brand-new car? A VCR? No. Do we have to spell everything out? We need to teach people to think for themselves! Lead them away from their mindless MTV states of being! Let them ponder the sociological ramifications of the naked nasal spray! They'll talk about it on the buses, they'll muse at the water coolers, they'll . . . it will inflame their tiny minds and override their stupefied senses! Then we'll follow it up with — something!! *(Beat. Kim stares at him.)* If we really need words, why don't we get them from her in our brainstorming session tomorrow? She just wants support. She needs reassurance. We listen and give her two thumbs up. It's all good. That's what she really wants. Does she not make us make it say what she wants it to say in the end anyway? Huh?! *(Kim is confused.)* Or we could come up with something like . . . now? *(Beat.)* I'm not stuck! I've never been stuck in my life! I'm just a little . . . blocked.

Red Salty Fluids
By Elaine M. Hazzard

Horace Grimaldi: twenty to thirty-nine, a worker of odd jobs, disk jockey and would be playwright. Horace is dashing, passionate, insecure, histrionic, obsessed, and potently sexy.

Comic

> *Horace, the newest member of a playwright group, is confronted by the group, after a brief reading of part of his play, with their concerns about practical staging problems in his play, not the least being the hacking of people to bits onstage and the eating of them. Horace addresses their criticism.*

HORACE: The concept? What is the concept of my play? It's, it's an irresistible urge. An urge that pushes up from the deep subconscious, flooding the personality with a drive stronger than lust, stronger than survival. So strong, the feelings of mortality, humanity and morality are burned away, a consuming passion, a desire to — *(Horace wants to bite imaginary meat before his mouth, then remembers where he is.)* You're all against me. Every one of you. You don't appreciate true art when you see it. I'm sorry I even brought my work here tonight, but I thought I'd give you another chance. I am not going to stay here and be insulted. No, no — don't try to stop me with words. I've heard all I want to hear. *(Horace storms out indignantly.)*

Personally Speaking
By Barbara Lhota and Janet B. Milstein

Dan: mid-twenties

Comic

> *Dan and Bess, twenties, are best friends on a quest to find their perfect mates. Every week they meet for brunch to discuss the "personals" date they went on the weekend before. Today, they meet to discuss their disastrous dates.*

DAN: I told you on the phone. *(Beat.)* "Blah." I mean, he was kinda cute when he came to my door. I definitely thought . . . "He's cute." So I showed him around my apartment, which he thought was great. And very manly. He said that — manly. Shut up! Don't laugh. So we decided to go to eat at Mario's and there were moments of uncomfortable silence when we were eating and I thought, "He has no personality at all. Here he gets to listen to people's problems all day long and he has nothing to say for himself. Has he no life? No interests? The least he could do is dish up some dirt about some old client whose confidentiality agreement has expired or something. But nooooo. . . he'd rather sit there in silence eating ravioli and listening to me gag on my meatball." Then I realize that the whole time I was thinking this thought, *I* was probably looking like *I'm* the one who appears to have no personality because I'm sitting here *thinking*. Then I thought, "Oh God, now I'm thinking this thought about thinking I have no personality, which is perpetuating this continued silence at the table. I've got to stop thinking thoughts and talk." So I took a sip of wine and said, "Do you like pigs?" I didn't know what to say. It was the first thing that came into my head. I just thought it would open up the conversation.

Personally Speaking
By Barbara Lhota and Janet B. Milstein

Dan: mid-twenties

Seriocomic

> *Dan and Bess, twenties, are best friends on a quest to find their perfect mates. Every week they meet for brunch to discuss the "personals" date they went on the weekend before. Today, they meet to discuss their disastrous dates.*

DAN: OK. So let's review. We both like breakfast. We're both broke. And I'm as Italian as Meryl Streep. Look, Bess, I think this personal ad thing is getting a little old. I've met twenty-nine guys! And I haven't had more than one date with any of them. It's been disastrous. My fourth date wanted me to meet his mother. The twenty-third took me to a folk-music-slash-poetry-slam. You can't know what you're going to get by reading a list of random attributes. "Barbra Streisand fan, enjoys yoga." He could mean that he heard a Barbra song once or that he plasters life-size posters of her all over his bedroom while saluting her sun. Besides, these "dates" create false expectation, more pressure, more weirdos. I think sometimes the old-fashioned meet-the-guy-at-the-bar-or-gym is the best way to go. Well bar. The point is that the personals set up a false, uncomfortable situation — a fabrication through words. You need to meet in person. *(Beat.)* So . . . Where's the next singles ten-minute dating thing? *(He looks at her.)* That's natural. You talk for ten minutes. You meet. You dump. Just like in the bar. You don't read about each other. It's more bang for your buck. Fifty dates in ten minutes. You just churn those rejects out. You can't lose!

The Voyage of the Carcass
By Dan O'Brien

Dan: twenties

Comic

Dan, a playwright, is having an affair with Helen, a married actor. She asks him to talk about when he first realized that he wanted to be a writer, and he answers her by telling a story that may or may not be entirely true.

DAN: . . . When I was a boy — maybe five, six years old — my parents took me to Quebec.

    We stayed in a Bed and Breakfast run by this exceptionally overweight Inuit woman . . .

    She was New Agey . . .

    She had Egyptian prints hung over each doorway. You know: "Glyphs." The furniture was like stage furniture, and the walls were painted deep red, blood color . . .

    I remember we were leaving for the night and it was very cold. We'd gotten all the way to the car before I realized I didn't have my mittens. I loved those mittens. My father gave me the key and told me to go back inside and get them myself. I was a big boy now.

    My heart was pounding in my neck. The house was dark and empty — . I opened the door to the room, and there, on my parents' bed, was the exceptionally overweight Inuit woman, having sex with a very small man . . .

    A dwarf maybe, or a midget. *(Pause.)*

    That's when I first realized I wanted to be a writer. *(Pause.)*

    Kind of makes sense though, doesn't it?

Dreaming of a White House
By Leanna Hieber

Dave: twenties, a lifelong slacker ready to clean up his act

Seriocomic

> *Dave, a lifelong slacker suddenly turned activist, earnestly*
> *tries to convince his ex-girlfriend not to leave town but to*
> *stay, marry him, and help his brand-new political campaign.*

DAVE: I'm here because I'm going to ask you to marry me. *(Beat. Excited.)* I'm gonna run for president in 2012, so I need a nice young wife to start building a watertight life with. The golden boy must begin young. What, you're looking at me like you think I'm kidding. C'mon, this is just the thing to do. Once you marry me, the seeds are planted. I see you arming the heat-seeking missiles of your eyes to shoot me down, but listen. I had a dream the night you left and it freaked me out. I dreamt everyone got cancer and we only had one month left. One month to do anything for ourselves, strangers, those we loved . . . And you know what? Nobody did a damn thing. Everyone sat weeping into beers. One big pity party, and then they all died. They dropped like flies on bar stools, in casinos, in dark alleyways and yeah, on their couches, whining. Scared the shit out of me. I don't wanna be that, Erin. So . . . here's the jump start we were waiting for. You didn't feel like waiting around 'til I figured it out, I see that. And you sure didn't waste time in moving on — REBOUND say I, but whatever — I'm telling you now, don't get on that plane. Seriously. Oh, YET . . . I know what you're thinking: "But Dave, where's room for all my kinky forays that I seek to pursue without you?" Well, you can whoop it up with "Reed" all you like, just be discreet. *(Beat.)* You don't really like that guy . . . do you?

Leave
By Matthew A. Everett

Seth: a tall, powerfully built man in his late twenties, a Marine

Dramatic

> *Seth is trying to explain to his civilian lover Nicholas why continuing a career in the Marines is so important to him. The distance and secrecy required by the military's "Don't ask, don't tell" policy have put a strain on their relationship but Seth thinks it might be worth it.*

SETH: I don't know, Pup. Before the Marines, it was just you and me. For years. Just us. And this town. I don't know, I got lost in "us" somehow. I didn't know who I was anymore. Just me. On my own. Apart from you. But I found out how strong I am. When I enlisted, I didn't know if I could do it. Even boot camp, just not being able to see you at the end of the day. I thought I'd die. But I didn't. I know who I am when I'm a Marine. I don't need to stop what I'm doing for college, to learn. I can take correspondence courses. I have. I am. But what I'm doin' right now is so important. I'm protecting the most important things on this earth — my country, my home, and you. I'm keepin' you safe, Nick. And people respect that. I've seen the world outside this town and these other people, they see me, apart from you, and they don't see some stupid loser with smudged hands and stained overalls, smellin' like gasoline. People see me all the time now the way I used to feel only when I was alone with you — clean and sharp and strong. Someone that matters. If the only thing I gotta do for that is learn how to write letters in code and live alone, maybe it's worth it. Except for loving you, being a Marine's the only thing I ever got right. It's the only thing that even comes close. *(Pause.)* I think I need this.

Bats
By N. M. Brewka

Kevin: a male of twenty

Dramatic

> *Kevin, a junior-college star catcher, begs his coach to let him play with a broken collarbone the day all the pro scouts appear.*

KEVIN: Jeez, come on, coach, please, you've got to let me play. It's just a bump, the doctors all said so. In fact, you know what? The doc in ER, he told me he sees this kind of shit, sorry, this kind of injury all the time, guys like painters, for instance, they fall off the roof and bam! But they go right back up there, because sitting around on your ass, oh, jeez, I mean, like, there's no treatment for it, you know? Like, you can't put your friggin' collarbone in a sling. You have got to let me play, coach. I don't have any pain. Honest.

Bats
By N. M. Brewka

Bert: a male of about twenty-eight

Dramatic

> *Baseball junior-college coach Bert calms down star-catcher*
> *Kevin after telling him he can't play for the pro scouts with*
> *a broken collarbone.*

BERT: Right. Go on, quit. Throw it all away. Shoot off your mouth
and march off with your head held high. Hey, at least you spoke
your mind. Got it all off your chest, didn't you, Kevin? Everything except the part about how hurt you really are inside, how
bad you feel about blowing it. You think I don't know how you
feel? Give me a break. Right now you're bleeding inside, blaming yourself, me and the entire universe for wrecking your
dream. All you did was play a little touch football and look how
you got punished. Yeah, right, the universe was just waiting to
screw our boy Kevin here, wars, disease, they don't count for
squat when it comes to suffering. No, Kevin here has it cornered.
You think I don't know how it feels? Everybody has a dream,
Kev. Yours just got delayed a little.

Bats
By N. M. Brewka

Rico: male, twenty

Seriocomic

Rico, junior-college star pitcher, comforts his best friend, catcher Kevin, after Kevin breaks a collarbone in practice the day before all the pro scouts are due.

RICO: So, this time it didn't work out. So what? Look at it as a little down time. Next year, those guys'll be back and you know what? You'll sign a contract for five mil, no, that's not enough, make it seven. OK, so you sign for seven, and you know with who. I mean, no doubt in my mind, you're going to the top, bro. Next year, you'll get another break, but it'll be the lucky kind. "Thank you, Mr. Steinbrenner," that's what you'll be saying, "and by the way, my ring size is ten and a half, and so is my dick." Right? Right.

The Size of the World
By Charles Evered

Peter Hogancamp: twenties, an ambitious young man from Passaic, New Jersey

Seriocomic

Peter explains to his boarders his philosophy of public speaking.

PETER: See the thing you have to remember when you're sayin' something you're not sure of, is to move onto the next thing you're sayin' as quick as possible, before the people you're talkin' to realize that you didn't have any idea what the thing you were just talkin' about meant. Do ya know what I'm sayin'? See this way, by the time you move onto the next thing, they've already forgotten about whatever it was you were just talkin' about — even though you had no idea what it was yourself. Now do ya know what I'm talkin' about? See it's better to say nothin' than to let people know you don't know what you're talkin' about. Remember, a person can be two things when they're not talkin': a genius, or a friggin' moron. And as soon as that person opens their mouth, they're automatically found out. Believe me, it's better to be thought of as a quiet genius than to be known as a somewhat gregarious moron with mediocre thoughts.

Al Capone and Me
By Ruth Tyndall Baker

Max: a wire mill worker, about twenty-four

Dramatic

Setting: Sparsely furnished one-room apartment, 1927– 1928. Max wants to buy the boarding house and is trying to convince Millie, his young wife, that they should.

MAX: *(To Millie.)* That boardin' house I used to live at? It's for sale. — Mr. Steven's is gonna lose it, Millie. He can't make the payments on it, and his house where he lives — it's almost paid for, and he says we can have the boardin' house if we just take over the payments. *(Beat.)* Here's the thing: We can keep the same boarders, but we'd have to put two more in the parlor; it has those sliding doors for privacy. If you'd be willing to cook for all of 'em, we could ask another dollar or so a week, and we could actually make enough for the house payment. *(Beat.)* It's up to you, Millie. It's more work for you than me. But you could quit the factory job. Stay at home. As soon as we have the car paid off, we'd stop boarding folks, and we could have the house all to ourselves. *(Silence.)* It wouldn't be any different than living in this one-room joint! We'd make the living room downstairs into our own apartment. The others have rooms upstairs. They're small, but there's five of them. . . . That house was sure built for a big family! . . . After supper dishes are done, we can go into our own room, shut the door and listen to the radio. *(Beat.)* If you want the house, I suppose we can go look at it on Sunday, but he's got to let it go real soon, and he'd rather let us have it than turn it back over to the bank. We don't have to if you don't want to . . . but with you at home, maybe we could start the family we want. What'd you think? You want to look at it? . . . Comes with people in it . . . And some day it'll be ours, and we'll have babies in it. *(Beat.)* You're the top banana, Millie; you know that?

Knock
By Lauren Kettler

Lem: early twenties. He'd be good ol' boy material if only he didn't think so dang much.

Seriocomic

Lem, a veritable fool for love, is trying to explain to a mutual friend of sorts why he tricked his blind girlfriend Miranda into believing that he shot himself.

LEM: Can you tell her that's all it was to begin with, a big old joke? That I was going to grab her then like I did just now and that was going to be the end of it? Only she was out the door before I could open my mouth and that's when it hit me. If Miranda was ever going to realize how much she cared, it was going to be right then and there, when she thought she'd really lost me. I had this gun, see, and Miranda here thought it was real. So when I started playing around with it, it made her plenty nervous. And I liked seeing her get all concerned over me. She never gets concerned over me, not the way you want your girl to get concerned. So I'm sitting there toying with this gun and I say to Miranda, I say, you want to be my wife? Which I been saying a lot of lately. 'Course she says no and it was the darnedest thing but the very next second we hear this gunshot. And let me tell you, it sounded close. I mean, in-the-room kind of close. I look at Miranda and I could see her every thought tattooed all over her pretty little face. She thought I went and shot myself. So I just lay there playing it up. I mean, what self-respecting prankster wouldn't, right? But I didn't do it to take advantage. What I did was take a shot, no pun intended. You know how they say that opportunity knocks? Well maybe sometimes what you find isn't exactly an opportunity. Maybe it's more like a door, and you have to knock for yourself. That's kind of what I did tonight, isn't it? I saw a door and I knocked.

Acceptance Letter
By Barbara Lhota and Janet B. Milstein

Charlie: young adult, a bit geeky

Dramatic

> *Charlie, a gifted student, has just discovered that his mother hid his college acceptance letter to a prestigious school out East. His mother, Tina, selfishly didn't want to say good-bye to him. He feels angry and hurt when he discovers her betrayal. In this speech, he reminds her that he has no choice but to leave. His dreams cannot be fulfilled unless he does.*

CHARLIE: One year? Maybe, maybe I could do it. Work at the paper mill. They need engineers. That's a challenging job. And engineers make a pretty good salary. Right? Then maybe the year turns into many. And I give up hope of ever being on the Genome project, or designing rockets that orbit Saturn, or creating technologies that defy the very laws of gravity! I know I'm weird. But I love trig! I love physics, and chemistry, and Latin! And Mom, I will invent something. I don't know what yet, but it'll be big, or part of something big. I have big expectations — huge, and yet, your expectations for me are so small. That's what I don't get. You say you love me, but you act as if you hardly knew me. Because if you did, you would know I could survive a four-year university. It's all I ever prepared for and dreamed of. And don't you see? You could leave Black River too! You, you can leave with me! We could get a place together. There are jobs in bowling alleys in Cambridge. They're probably tons. What do you say?! *(Pause.)* All these years you've had me fooled. You always pretended to be such a wild free-spirit. Margarita parties at Christmas. Yeah. The party girl who would do anything, go anywhere if only she had more money and less kid. The truth is that you're afraid of anything outside of here, aren't you? But I need to meet people more like me. I can't stay here with you just because you want me to. Can't you see that? It'll destroy me.

MacKenzie
By John Michael Manship

Connor: mid-twenties, a small-time entrepreneur

Dramatic

> *Connor has discovered the rumor of a poltergeist in a local cemetery that is said to bruise, cut, and even knock out passerbys. He wants to exploit these stories and needs the support of his roommate and friend, David. In response, David suggests that if the poltergeist is real, then the tour is a bad idea. Connor disagrees.*

CONNOR: No. Then we're the luckiest people on earth. Because — inside these walls was a person, just like you or I, living in a different time or place but very much the same as either of us. This person has died, probably in some tragic and frightening way. This person has shuffled off this mortal coil and turned to dust and yet — here he is, back again, gripping people by the throats, leaving bruises on arms and legs, feeling and being felt. Do you see what I'm getting at? What we're witnessing here is a break in the laws of not only death but of life. It's a cheat sheet. It makes faith irrelevant. This creature is connected to the great unknown, call it the energy of the universe, the mysterious power, the numinous. Call it God if you want to — pardon me if I don't. My friend, if this thing touches you, you have proof-positive witnessed something there is absolutely no way to prove. Ironic, isn't it? Hundreds of people suffered here for their religion. Thousands more elsewhere throughout time, dying in crusades and quests and all that silly shit, just to get a glimpse of truth. And we're offering it for just ten quid. Answers, to life's deepest questions. Gather round, tour group, and follow me into this ancient mysterious cemetery . . .

Critical Acclaim
By John Michael Manship

Devin: twenty-one, a psychology student

Dramatic

> *Kathryn is infatuated with Devin's artistic talents and those of his father, a successful painter. Devin avoids both subjects relentlessly and Kathryn wants to know why. Finally, she gets her answer when her accusation that Devin is "wasting" his talent ignites this cathartic monologue about "the voice."*

DEVIN: Once someone sees your very first creation, it appears. It's barely a whisper. It congratulates you, quietly in the back of your head. It does that for years, rewarding you for your efforts. Later it speaks to you, aloud, and comforts you when you fear your work is worthless. It saves you from having to feel bad about your creation. Of course, you listen. It grows rapidly louder, but its tone changes. It draws focus. It pushes you to be better. You continue to accept it, allowing it to become a bigger and bigger part of you, open to the idea that through obedient attention, you are somehow learning to create. Finally, if you let it, it consumes your thoughts altogether. Soon that voice, once comforting, is a constant, unwelcome companion, a cancer on your creativity. But really, it always was. Why? The moment you heard that voice, you accepted that your creation can be ranked and quantified. The voice I'm talking about says something in your creation can be *wrong,* in which case you must make it *better;* that what you create isn't beautiful unless it is beautiful enough. And that voice doesn't just belong to you. It belongs to us all, constantly. It screamed the first time you got here. I heard it when you first noticed my paintings. And I listened. For that moment, it was all I could hear. Worse, for that moment, I became the voice to you. I looked at you through the eyes of both of our fathers. Don't listen, Kathryn. To listen is to stain. To listen is to waste.

The Train in My Hotel
By Mary Portser

Tony: a New York actor in his twenties or thirties, cocky, but freaking out in this scene

Comic

Tony and Carol are New York actors who've gone to the sticks for a job. They've just found out the town they're in has a shockingly high homicide rate. Tony, who's very attracted to Carol, comes to her hotel room, seeking comfort.

TONY: Thanks for letting me in, Carol. I've got to talk to you about something serious. This hotel is toxic. Have you tasted the water here? You can taste the cancer in it. The food. More grease than a Brylcream bottle. That Mario is out to kill everyone he comes in contact with. We're seven miles from the supermarket, Carol. We take our lives into our hands every time we go to the car. In the car, we're seven miles of sitting duck. And what about the air? The air we're breathing? We can't open the windows. We're hermetically sealed. *(He tries to open a window.)* Look at that. Think of the bacteria trapped in here with us. Then there's the seventh floor — which I might add — is directly above us. The elevator doesn't stop at the seventh floor. I asked the guy at the desk and he mumbled something about the help using it. Doesn't that strike you as strange? The help are locals. They go home at night to their dangerous hovels. What goes on up there? I've heard noises. Christ, we were so much safer back in New York. I don't know if I can take much more of this. Can I get into bed with you?

The Fundraiser
By Dan Stroeh

Len: late twenties to early thirties, a "visual artist" from New York City, Agoraphobic, Obsessive-Compulsive, depressed, who knows what else

Comic

> *In the abandoned auditorium adjacent to a theater company's yearly fundraiser, highly neurotic Len, desperate for solitude, seeks a moment of peace and quiet. Just as he begins a "cleansing exercise" to deal with his agoraphobia, Maddy sneaks in to wait for a passionate rendezvous with a visiting actor from Columbia. Here Len explains his cleansing exercise.*

LEN: It's not a hot dog, it's a frank. In fact, it's not even a frank, it's an exercise. A cleansing exercise. My psychiatrist says that it is important for me to have a cleansing exercise to take part in when I spend time outside of my apartment. When I am at parties, like this one, I have a tendency to feel overwhelmed. To have panic attacks and pass out. A cleansing exercise would curb this a little, my psychiatrist said. Whenever I feel overwhelmed or anxious, I simply excuse myself to a quiet room and begin my cleansing exercise. Yes, I realize that it's a bit strange, but it is important to be honest with oneself when choosing a cleansing exercise. One must pick the thing that calms one the most. Eating franks calms me. And before you ask, yes. I am gay. And no, it's not the shape. To be completely honest, the semi-phallic nature of the frank has nothing to do with my choosing it as my cleansing exercise. If anything, the shape . . . disturbs me.
(Beat.)
Now, as we agreed, I told you about my franks, and I would appreciate it very much if you would leave me alone.

Throwing Stones in Glass Houses
By Kevin Schwendeman

Howard: twenty-eight, obsessive-compulsive, views everything in
   black and white

Comic

> *Howard, an uptight obsessive-compulsive, finds himself in*
> *an adulterous marriage. After discovering his wife has*
> *cheated on him, Howard visits St. Francis church, which is*
> *holding a help group called Yes! Life. At the beginning of the*
> *play each character says a bit about themselves, paralleling*
> *the beginnings of such meetings. Howard, unable to say*
> *anything in small detail, fires off a fast-paced tangent*
> *regarding culinary dos and don'ts. This tangent parallels his*
> *views of the basic inherent rules in life. His quick pace of*
> *thought often leads him down logic chains that tend to be*
> *disregarded and defined as metaphoric babble. However, his*
> *conviction leads us to believe there is sanity somewhere in*
> *what he says.*

HOWARD: I asked for a glass of water and when it comes it's in this
   tiny little glass with more ice than a glass of that size should be
   able to hold. There was so much ice that I only got two drinks
   of actual water out of the glass. So you ask, "Why not just wait
   for the ice to melt?" I'll tell you. Because melted ice water has
   been through one too many molecular, physical state of being
   changes or whatever. It's not the same. The difference in taste is
   so — different. It's like Miracle Whip and mayonnaise. Do *not*
   get these two mixed up. It is wrong to call Miracle Whip mayo.
   I mean right on the bottle it says "salad dressing." And I don't
   like salad dressing on my sandwiches. Miracle Whip doesn't
   even have mayo in it. But do you know what it does have in it?
   Mustard flour. Now if there is anything that doesn't belong in a
   mayonnaise wannabe, it's mustard flour. There is nothing more
   different from mayonnaise than mustard. But mustard is OK. I
   like mustard on my sandwiches. But not in my potato salad. I've
   seen it. Mustard potato salad. You don't see mayonnaise on hot

dogs do you? No, because mayonnaise is too classy. Only mustard can be so pretentious. It's a war. A full-scale, well-calculated condiment war and it's going on right before our very eyes! Ranch dressing on French fries! No! It's against every law of nature! That is ketchup's responsibility. The excuse? "It tastes better." No. There are certain laws that are not to be broken. Certain lines that can't be crossed. Ever. Anyway . . . that's why I never order water at restaurants.

October Rose
By Terri Campion

Eric Talbot: mid-twenties, a stressed-out banker, saddled with a wife
   and child much too early in his life

Seriocomic

*Eric undergoes an interrogation for the murder of an erotic
masseuse who he was seeing several times a week.*

ERIC: What are you kidding me? I invented jerking off. It's OK for
   temporary relief. But every night? In the bathroom like some
   perv. I had to start using magazines, hiding them in the toilet
   tank in plastic bags. Eventually they stopped working and it's
   taking longer and longer. I'm in there forty-five minutes, an hour,
   hour and a half. That's too much time to be spending on yourself! We just had a baby, and Ceely, my wife she's just not into
   it. A few weeks she keeps telling me. I'm a horny guy! That's
   why I joined that stupid gym. I was trying to divert my energy.
   But this one day I'm on the ski machine and there's this class
   going on in the exercise room right in front of me. And it's filled
   with all these girls. And they're doing this kinda dancey aerobics,
   and they're wearing these outfits that are kinda sexy but not
   slutty. And some are tall and skinny and some are small and a
   little chubby, but they all have nice butts, and pony tails all different shades of blond and brown. And they're dancing in sync
   with each other and laughing and sweating and having a good
   time! And . . . *(Breaks down.)* and I want to hold them! I want
   to take them in my arms and pull the scrungies out of their pony
   tails and run my fingers through their hair and taste their sweat
   and feel their hearts pounding! I just want a three-dimensional
   woman! I didn't kill her! Why would I kill her? I loved
   seeing her.

Broken Peaces
By Jeannine Coulombe

Jaret: late twenties

Comic

After being given a lawn rooster by his annoying neighbor, Jaret smashes the gift to pieces. His wife enters and inquires about his behavior. Jaret can hardly control his anger as he explains his actions.

JARET: What am I doing? I'm letting off steam. That's what I'm doing. That darn neighbor of ours just gave me this piece of shit lawn rooster to stick on our lawn. Yeah. I smashed it. I smashed it good. I don't want a lawn rooster. You understand? I don't want it. I hate lawn ornaments! There are two kinds of people in this world — those who like lawn ornaments and those who don't. I don't. That's that. But look over there. Look at that man's yard. He has every kind there is — the classic gnome, the flamingo, the guy fishing off the pier, the rabbit, the rooster, the windmill. And then the not-so-nice ones — that woman bending over showing off her panties and that guy peeing into some pond or another. What's that all about? They're ugly. Not cute, not quaint and sure to hell not decorative. Just plain ugly. And he's got 'em strewn all over the place. Up the side of his driveway, willy-nilly on his lawn, some hidden in the bushes. Look, he's even got one on the roof of his garage. And he moves 'em around. What's that all about? They're just plain ugly no matter where he puts 'em. But I always figured as long as he keeps them off my property there wasn't much I could do about them. But now he went and gave me one. Where does he get off? I know what he's trying to do, he's trying to take over our lawn, that's what he's up to. But I'm not going to let him. Oh, no! I smashed it. I smashed it good. He's gotta be stopped! He's taking over! He's gotta be stopped!!!

Law-V-Bow-Em
By Dan Stroeh

Henry: mid-twenties, a writer (sort of), obsessed with books, rarely leaves his chair in which he "reads" continuously, sleeps there as well, very active imagination

Comic

Henry, Trent, and H are roommates living in New York's East Village, trying to live the life of the Bohemian even though they have no talent whatsoever. Here Henry responds to H's question, "Have you seen Himmel Uber Berlin?"

HENRY: No, H, I have not seen *Himmel Uber Berlin.* You know I do not watch your mind-numbing movies. You know that as a man of literary integrity I refuse to subject myself to the intellectual genocide that this nation's entertainment industry is systematically conducting throughout the world. You know how I feel about the very presence of that idiot box and its friends in this apartment, and if it weren't for the fact that you were here before me and you pay most of the rent, I would INSIST, on a moral and intellectual basis, that they be removed from the vicinity and cast into a fiery furnace much like Shadrach, Meshack, and Abednego. You are very well aware of my deep concern that their proximity to my books may be influencing me negatively and that they could, in fact, be poisoning my thought process, perhaps irreversibly, simply by being so close to my books and my brain. Osmosis! Osmosis is a very real and frightening thing and I worry about it, H, I really do.
(He breathes.)
So, no. No, I have not seen *Himmel Uber Berlin.*

From Where I Stand
By Jason Furlani

Donny: twenties, the extremely loyal and somewhat manic best friend of Jim, his lifelong buddy, who is now engaged to Donny's younger sister. Donny manages his family's Italian restaurant in Schenectady, N.Y.

Comic

Jim and Donny are lifelong friends. Having received an urgent phone call from Jim, Donny has dropped everything and rushed to Jim's apartment, located in the very "inconvenient" Stockade section of Schenectady, N.Y. Here Donny is caught between impatiently wanting to "fix" whatever's wrong, and the toils of being a good friend.

DONNY: Sorry it took me so long; got here as soon as I could. As usual, Doc MacConnell's got his son-of-a-bitch Cadillac takin' up half the fuckin' block. I hadda circle around like eighteen — no wait! (One, two, fifteen —) Nineteen! Nineteen times, round and round and round. Got so dizzy I almost puked. (I shoulda. Shoulda puked. Right on shit-head Doc MacConnell's windshield!) So finally — See how fast he gets his chicken parm next time he's down the restaurant — So finally, I wound up — hadda park over on goddamned Jay Street and hike it up scumbag alley there. Oh-ho-ho what a trip! All the places in Schenectady you could live you gotta be in the one neighborhood nobody's got a driveway. And I know — I know it's "historic." Whatever! What, driveways ain't historic? I mean, ya figure the Forefather's woulda layed down a couple driveways for like their horses or some shit, ain't it? Whaddya gonna do, hook yer horse up on the street there? I wouldn't. Doc MacConnell'd mow it down with that big bastard boat a his!

(*Then.*) You ain't lookin' so good. You eat today?

(*Then.*) Eh. Who knows maybe they put all the horses over on Jay Street there. Maybe that's why it stinks so fuckin' bad. I swear, one a those little punks keys my car — I SWEAR! EH. It's fine. I'm sure it's fine. It's fine. So, anyway, you called, I'm here. Here I am. What's up?

Lone Star Grace
By Suzanne Bradbeer

Kenneth Fannin: twenties

Comic

> *Kenneth has driven all the way from New Jersey to Texas to visit the battleground where his ancestor was killed. Having stopped for breakfast in a small Texas diner, he has just been confronted by a very flirtatious but intimidating Texas bombshell.*

KENNETH: I came in here for some peace and quiet, for a relaxed breakfast before I start my day, and what do I get: talk, talk, talk. I came in here to read my Atlas and plan my affairs and what do I get: talk, talk, talk. Talk, talk, talk, talk, talk. "Do you want your sausage?" Of course I want my sausage. That's why I ordered it. I ordered my sausage because I thought there was a good chance I'd want to eat my sausage, and now my sausage is cold. Talk, talk, talk. Blah, blah, blah. Barbie this and Houston that. Cucarachas, and coffee on my pants. Big hair and long legs. I am the great-great-great-grand nephew of Colonel James Walker Fannin who was murdered with his men in the bloodiest massacre of the Texas War for Independence. *Bloodier than the Alamo.* But does anyone ever talk about Colonel Fannin and the sacrifice he made? No, it's Davy Crockett this and Sam Houston that; San Antonio Rose and George W. Bush. Well I am going to the Fannin Battleground State Historic Park to pay my respects to the spirit of my great-great-great-grand uncle and I don't want to know about Barbie doll rabbit's foots, Macy's Department Store, or Bra School Training. So just say Happy Birthday to me and leave me alone.

Cat-tastrophy
By Barbara Lhota and Janet B. Milstein

Mathew: late twenties, a newlywed

Comic

> *Mathew and Bridget are newlyweds. They moved into their new home six months ago. So did their cats. Bridget and Mathew love each other. However, Bridget's two cats hate Mathew's cat. For six months now Bridget and Mathew have been trying everything possible to make them get along, including following a structured and laborious routine given to them by their cat therapist. It is now the middle of the night, and, once again, Mathew has been woken up by the cats fighting. He can't take it anymore.*

MATHEW: Yes. We've done the group therapy. We've played classical music to soothe them. Family activity time. Creating self-space and seclusion for each of them. We've kept our play dates. We even drugged them! But it didn't work. It didn't work. Our cats cannot live together! Maybe our cats just hate each other? Ever think of that? And besides, I was very united, even when you weren't. It was me who made sure everyone had Friskie treats at all merging times, right? I'm the one who had to spread the pheromones all over — me. You act as if you're the only one who bore the brunt of this. And it's kind of hard to be "affectionate" when your cats are under your bed, ripping each other's ears off, isn't it? It's hard to concentrate on making love when they're going *(Imitating the screech.)* "Reeooooooowwww!" as they lunge over you and draw blood from your back as they graze it. Or listening to them knock every precious thing you've ever owned off the mantle. You saw them. They even dangled from the beads on the ugly lamp. Not that your grandmother's antique lamp is ugly. See what's happening here? They're pitting us against each other. We can't keep pointing fingers at each other. This is the beginning of our life together and they are tearing us apart! We got very ugly last night. Very, very ugly. Uglier than we've ever been. Minus the co-construction of the Ikea bookcase and the mounting-the-bike-rack incident. We wanted this very badly, but it just can't go on. I think you know it as well as I. We must *(Sighs.)* separate the cats.

felling giants
By Joshua Scher

Danny: twenty-five, a tough logger kid from a small town in the Pacific N.W.

Seriocomic

> *Danny is at the local watering hole with his friend Mark, Mike (Mark's almost mythical older brother), and Jake who is back for the first time in ten years. The conversation has turned tense as Mike has pressed Jake for why he's come home. Danny tries to distract the group with one of his most recent problems.*

DANNY: I got somethin that's been botherin' me all week. It's nothing really, just . . . I ah, well. I don't know, I've been getting all frustrated like cause, well cause, I can't stop smellin the inside of my nose. It's driving me crazy. *(Jacob starts laughing.)* I'm serious. It's fucking annoying, I mean I try not to notice, but it's right there every time I breathe. I even tried breathing through my mouth for a while, but that doesn't work cause eventually I slip and take a whiff through my nose, and there's the smell again and I get all flustered and conscious about it and then what. I can't do a friggin' thing cause it's all I can focus on. *(They all laugh, Mike gets up.)* You guys never get it. Seriously. Fuck. I can't stop thinking about it. Which is a problem when. . . you know . . . she's getting all hot and steamy and playful, and with all the heavy breathin' all I'm thinking about is how to stop smellin' the inside of my nose. It keeps me up at night too. And I know what you're thinking, you're thinking, "You can't smell the inside of your nose!" But I tell you, I can and I do. It's right there where you smell and all. Why can't you smell it?

The Age of Cynicism
or Karaoke Night at The Hog
By Keith Huff

Gary: twenties

Seriocomic

Gary is out on a really horrid blind date with Ellen, a sexually outspoken feminist.

GARY: You know, I'm really heartened to see feminism has had such a positive impact on women today. My mother burned her Playtex Cross My Heart bra for you. Do you appreciate the sacrifice? Do you seize the opportunities presented to you by those before you to maybe maternalize and soften a hard-edged, paternalistic, and bellicose world? No, you insult my mother and the ashes of her bra by coopting every sophomoric, pigpen behavior that was once the exclusive domain of men. You know who comes on strong? Skunks. *Skunks.* They come on strong to be repellent. They repel things they fear. That's what I think you're all about. Deep down I think you're a terrified little girl doing your shrieking all to keep the world and everything in it at bay.

I Ate Lunch Alone Today
By David-Matthew Barnes

Daniel: late twenties, a Bohemian, sensitive artist

Dramatic

> *Daniel has just come to terms with his unrequited love for Margaret, his next-door neighbor. Here he confesses his love for her and tries to convince her to end the relationship she is having with an overbearing man.*

DANIEL: Listen to me, Margaret. He has no idea how wonderful you are. He doesn't appreciate you. You're the most incredible woman I have ever known. You deserve more than this. You deserve love letters and poetry, slow dances in the rain, long passionate kisses that make your soul tingle. You deserve a man who tells you every day how much he loves you and how beautiful you are, that he would be lost without you. You need someone who is able to see heaven in your eyes and forever in your smile. I get lost in my thoughts about you, Margaret. Sometimes I sit in my apartment and I wish we were together. And I hear words through the wall — harsh words, unkind and ugly things that he says to you. And I hear you cry. Every day, you cry, Margaret and it tears me up inside. *(Beat.)* Let me love you. Let me give you the life that you deserve. If you do, I swear, you will never be alone again.

Rock Shore
By Lisa Dillman

McDade: twenty, the handyman at a tuberculosis sanatorium

Dramatic

*The year is 1913. In this monologue McDade reveals to his
critically ill girlfriend that he has contracted tuberculosis.*

MCDADE: I ain't ever felt about anybody the way I feel about you. I
think about you all day long sometimes. I think about your face
and how ya laugh. And the way your neck looks stickin' out of
your collar like that. The way you smell. All flowery. Little
things you say to me. I don't know. You probably got a whole
pile of fellas waitin' on ya back home, huh? *(Beat.)* What I was
gonna say before . . . I'll tell you. But you can't tell nobody else.
Swear? *(Beat.)* I got it too now. I got one side feels ten pounds
heavier'n the other. And every time I pull a deep breath I can
hear it and feel the catch. Listen. *(He draws a deep breath.)*
We're the same now, you and me. My mama died of it while
she's sucklin' me. I didn't get it then. I took this job and I been
face-to-face with TBs every single day since I's twelve. That's
almost eight years. And I never got it till now. Don't that tell you
something? *(Beat.)* Means we were put here for each other. I
ain't scared. This is what was meant to be. Tell me you think
so too.

If This Isn't Love
By Jonathan Bernstein

Hank: twenty-four, a part-time college student and test subject for pharmaceutical research

Comic

Smitten by Katie, a girl he met at a party this past weekend, Hank shows up at Katie's real estate office to ask her on a date.

HANK: Hi uh Katie? . . . Katie hi I'm Hank Matthews we met the other night at Jerry's party? . . . Hi. I — How are you how are things? . . . Good. Good. It's nice here I've never been here. OK — I'm just going to — Katie, I asked Jerry to tell me where you work and I'm not here following you in a scary way or anything, I just I have a question for you but first what I want to say is that since we met, Katie, since we met I can't get you out of my mind. I literally — you're stuck there — and meeting you the other night made me think that you and I have a lot of things in common to talk about and I know this is *forward* of me but I'd like to start talking with you about these things as soon as possible. So is there even the slightest fraction of an outside chance that you would ever consent to share eating dinner with me?, that's my question, because there's no way I could ever think of a way that I'd rather have dinner than with you. . . . "Sure" meaning yes you will? Are you sure? You don't have to. . . . You were thinking about me? *Me?* . . . Jesus. Me too. I was thinking about you, too. Jesus Christ, Katie, me too.

Thoughts and Remembrance
By Jennifer Miller

Josh: twenty-three years old, attractive, actor

Dramatic

> *Josh and Bern met in a philosophy class. Josh is a quiet, unassuming, but promising actor. Josh, an only child, has been lonely since childhood and is attracted to Bern who appears daring, bold, and irreverent. They've been going out long enough for Josh to realize he's falling in love with her. In this scene, Bern has just seen Josh perform for the first time. She is very impressed. They are sitting outside the theater killing time before a peace rally starts. Josh wants to skip the rally and go back to his place. Josh is hungry for Bern and wants to express his love.*

JOSH: A brother would have been OK, but a sister would have been more into the stuff I was into. I didn't like sports. My dad kept buying me baseball bats and soccer balls. I was more into books and art. Even my one friend thought I was weird. And my parents thought I was gay because I was always putting on makeup and dressing up. I wanted a real live sister to play dress up with. Somebody besides my imaginary friends and my mirror. I got tired of talking to that mirror. Then you walked in front of the class looking tough and terrified. You were so real. I knew I had to talk to you. And now you're here beside me. I don't have to imagine anymore. I can reach out and touch you. I want to taste your sweet and salty skin. I thought I knew everything until I met you.

Sloe Gin Fizz
By David-Matthew Barnes

Christopher: twenties

Dramatic

> *On a rainy night, two male co-workers, Marco and Christopher, are drawn together out of loneliness. Christopher is suffering from a broken heart after another failed relationship. Here, he talks about his true feelings for Marco.*

CHRISTOPHER: When I first saw you at work, it's like a part of me knew we would end up in this moment — with Sloe Gin on our breath and the rain outside and all these words and feelings. I saw all of this in you the second that I looked into your eyes. I can't explain it — but I knew that I was supposed to meet you and I knew that we were supposed to be together — I knew that we needed each other. And I would watch you — and how you flirted with all the girls at work and how easily you could talk to the guys and hang out with them. But I knew that really wasn't you. I knew that behind all of it was this guy who was just as lonely as me. And all I wanted to do was to hold you — and tell you not to worry anymore because everything was going to be all right. At first I was nervous to talk to you — I don't know if you realized it or not — but the first few times we spoke, I couldn't look you in the eye. Of course I've thought about what you would look like, standing in front of me naked and all that stuff — but more importantly, I imagined what it would be like just to be near you. But then I would go to work and I would lose my nerve. I would overhear you talking about your wife with the guys. I watched you with Lisa at the snack bar and those damn free hot dogs. And I couldn't do it. So many times I just wanted to walk right up to you and say, "Marco, I don't care what you try to tell these people. I know who you really are. *(Beat.)* And I think that I'm in love with you."

Sloe Gin Fizz
By David-Matthew Barnes

Marco: twenties

Dramatic

> *On a rainy night, two male co-workers, Marco and Christo-*
> *pher, are drawn together out of loneliness. Marco is married*
> *to a Korean woman whom he does not love. Here, he imag-*
> *ines what a relationship would be like with Christopher.*

MARCO: What if I walked you home every night? What if we went
out to dinner? What if we went away on a weekend trip? What
if I moved in here with you and I was faithful and I was good to
you and I treated you with respect and I taught you to believe in
forever again? What if I took you by the hand right now and
pulled you into my arms and allowed myself to make love to you
until the sun came up and then in the morning, we would have
breakfast together, take a shower and wash each other's backs
and drive to work together. And when work was done, we came
home together and we had dinner and then watched television
and talked until we fell asleep in each other's arms. And from
every day forward, I promised you that you would never feel
alone again. Would you believe me, Christopher? Would you let
me love you like that? And would you love me back — just as
much — with your whole heart and soul? *(Beat.)* I love you. My
God, sometimes I wish I didn't. I wish I could go home to my
wife and make love to her with the passion that I feel for you. I
wish I could be the guy that my friends all think that I am. I wish
that I could wake up tomorrow morning and never be scared
again.

Limping Towards Babylon
By Julius Galacki

Marcus: mid to late twenties. Currently in grad school, he's a man of intelligence, loyalty and sensitivity. While not overly handsome, he's pleasant enough looking. Unfortunately, being his own worst enemy, he wears the Scarlet *L* of loser on his forehead. Thus, amongst other aspects of his life, romance has been rather sporadic.

Comic

In this scene, Marcus is trying to persuade his best friends, Paul and Jimmy, that he has met the One, the woman he is fated for.

MARCUS: Um, well, Jimmy and I were at 8 BC having a beer and this enormous guy from nowhere says, "Don't point at me." That's what he said. I didn't even know I was pointing. Then I . . . I don't know. I kinda' fell. I tripped on something. . . . That's not the fate part. This is. I'm on the ground in what should just be another humiliating experience and then I see this purple sandal. . . . No, just her shoe. It somehow had fallen off her foot. So I forget all about the big angry guy and I'm crawling on the floor looking for a naked foot. Then there it is, an arch like . . . from a cathedral. Maybe with some dirt on it. But the line was perfect. It lifted me up, straight to her face. . . . I don't even remember what her body looked like. But her hair was like flax. It glowed. I held the sandal in offitorio. . . . it's not important if it's a real word. What matters is her smile was real and it was for me . . . She said "Thanks." Then, *I* said, "I think you're beautiful." I don't just say that kind of stuff to a stranger. You know that! But it just came out of my mouth. . . . Uh, well, that's when the bouncers threw us out. . . . But these are the kind of fateful encounters that cannot be ignored. She was a vision. . . . Jimmy, you didn't even see her. You were busy fighting that guy for me. . . . I put an ad in the back page of the *Village Voice*. "Cinderella. You lost your shoe. I gave it back to you. Let's meet again." . . . I tell you, this one is different.

The Pinnacle
By Barbara Lhota and Janet B. Milstein

Lincoln: twenty-eight, a nervous sort

Seriocomic

> *For several months, Lincoln has been planning to ask Liz to marry him, but he wanted a proper setting in which to ask. He has planned a romantic getaway to Italy to pop the question. The only problem is that Lincoln has lost the engagement ring. He suspects the hotel maid of stealing it, so he's been complaining to the management and obsessed with trying to locate this maid. Liz, not knowing his plan, is feeling hurt and fiercely angry because Lincoln has been ignoring her throughout the entire vacation. He is constantly talking to his friends in the nearby villa, and acting like an idiot. In this scene, Lincoln has taken Liz to a romantic Italian restaurant to pop the question. Liz wants to break up with him.*

LINCOLN: No, no. I was nervous. I was really nervous and going over and over it in my head — my speech. I was really going to ask me to marry you tonight. Urgh, you to marry me. That's why I was picky about the restaurant. That's why my friends weren't talking to you. They were nervous. They were nervous for me. Didn't know how I was going to ask. See, I kept changing how I was going to ask you, finding better, more beautiful sites. And then the whole ring thing. Who knew that would happen? Her stealing the ring. And then everybody said just ask her tonight — ring or not! And then we're late! God, I love you. *(Sighs.)* That's all I wanted to say. It seems easy. I love you. Will you marry me?

The House at the Edge of the World
By Richard Zinober

Perry DePrima: twenty-five, a truck driver, a lover, and a fighter

Seriocomic

> *Perry met Ann, a resident in a halfway house working as a waitress at a diner, shortly before her anxiety disorder worsened and she stopped coming to work. He has wheedled her address from a co-worker and come to the halfway house to ask her out on a date.*

PERRY: Picture it from my point of view, will you? There I am, driving produce into the city just about every night of my life for the past five years — a job that can get kind of lonely with all those hours on the road. 'Cause that's all my life is, 'cept when I'm sleeping: me in the cab and the night out there, just these pairs of headlights coming toward me and these pairs of taillights moving along ahead of me. I hardly ever see another person's face, unless somebody's lighting a cigarette while I'm passing them. So it's nice, when I got half an hour to myself, to stop at this diner where it's all lit up bright and sit next to other people and hear them talking and sipping coffee. It's even nice for a change to smell somebody else's body odor. Then one night there's this new waitress who's cute and kind of crazy — in a good way, I mean. And all of a sudden the diner ain't just a place to take a break. I'm sitting at the counter, drinking coffee and listening to the funny, crazy things she says, and when she's down at the other end, serving some other customer, I'm just watching her and thinking what I'm gonna say next. And life ain't so bad all of a sudden. 'Cause even though I only get to see her half an hour a day, I'm thinking about her all the time now — on the road, at home, before I go to sleep at night. It's the same life, but completely different. Everything's changed. Then one night I show up and find out you're sick — or *something* — and maybe you're never coming back. How do you think that makes me feel? You got any idea what it took to find you — to get Cheryl to give me this address? *(Beat.)* Look, I ain't asking you to go back to work. All I came here for is to ask you out. You know, to a movie or something. What do you say, Ann?

Birdsend
By Keith Huff

Bird: twenties or thirties

Seriocomic

> *Bird is schizophrenic. Margie, a former girlfriend, has*
> *shown up at his apartment broke and pregnant. In this*
> *scene, Bird attempts to persuade Margie to stay with him.*

BIRD: Cook County Hospital, they made me take a psychological evaluation. Lady wanted me to talk about flying. But I talked about you mostly. I told her "Margie, she's so beautiful. I look in her eyes, I see through, another world, world where people don't fight, lie, smell, die. I see a place: all this light, the sun I missed, possibility. Place a man like me can grow wings and soar!"
(Pause.)
     She referred me to a specialist.
(Pause.)
     But you *are* beautiful, Margie. I don't mean beauty you see. That beauty sags, sinks, stinks, rots, it drips off the bone. That beauty dies. I mean beauty inside you. You're a good person, Margie. That goodness in you, it's not something you touch. Not something you make love to. It's something you feel with your eyes and touch with your soul and makes you wanna rise up and fly away!

You Been Lied To
By Barbara Lhota and Janet B. Milstein

Jack: young adult

Dramatic

Jack just found out from a stranger that the woman he thought was his sister his whole life was really his biological mother.

JACK: Well, I'm ready to hear this explanation. Cause this is the most screwed up thing ever. I mean, here I am just hangin' out on my porch one day. Life's as it always is, and some dude starts telling me he went to high school with my mom. I'm thinkin' he means my sister — he's talkin' about you, not Edith — cause he's your age. So I'm not listening all that well — thinkin' about something else. Then he says, "So how is your mom? Is she as hot as she always was?" I want to pop him in the face, but I'm totally confused at the same time. My mom's about fifty years old, so I don't think she was ever hot to him. And if she was, I want to throw up. I say, "I'm confused," and he starts laughing. I tell him that he must have things backwards because my mom's around fifty, but he tells me I'm wrong. He says he knew my mom Pam from high school. She got pregnant like eighteen years ago. She got around with a lot of guys he says. He says *her* mother, Edith, was not pregnant. He notices that I look about eighteen. He laughs. "Get it?" He says. "Get what I'm sayin'?" I grabbed his shirt — suddenly, like outta nowhere, I just start poppin' him good ones. He didn't even see them coming. He pushes me hard. And I'm laying there. He spits and says real dramatic, "You been lied to, boy." Laughs. *(Beat.)* And I feel like my brain was just put in a blender.

MacKenzie
By John Michael Manship

David: mid-twenties, a graduate student

Dramatic

> *David wants nothing more than to be "touched" by the MacKenzie poltergeist, a spirit said to bruise, sicken, and even knock out those who encounter it. To David, being "touched" would be like a blessing from the divine: An affirmation that, despite what everyone says, he is significant and sane. Ironically, the poltergeist seems to avoid him, on this night choosing to "touch" his skeptical girlfriend, Carol, right before David's eyes. Her firm denial of the encounter sends him over the edge.*

(The gate. David walks out, a drink mostly empty in his hand. He walks to the gate, which is chained closed. He touches it, runs his hands along it. He sets the drink down, and grabs the gate, begins to pull, testing the chain and lock.)

DAVID: Chained in there good, eh? I know how you feel. Here's to you, Mr. MacKenzie. Here's to your health. You awake in there? I don't believe in things like you, you know. Don't listen to Carol. I don't believe. You hear me? I DON'T BELIEVE IN YOU! LISTEN TO ME! Oh, Jesus. *(He laughs. He holds the pill bottle in front of him, contemplates it for a long time, finally lets it roll off his hand onto the ground. He throws his head back to lean against the gate.)* You touched her. You put your hand on her shoulder and she doesn't even believe in you. She's in there, right now, sleeping soundly, because she isn't haunted by this feeling. You made her cold, and sick, and still she doesn't believe in you. How does that make you feel? *(He starts to laugh again.)* Jesus. You're not even real, you asshole! You're not even real! Touch me. Touch me. Come on. If you're real, then touch me. TOUCH ME! MAKE ME COLD! I DARE YOU GOD DAMNIT MAKE ME COLD! Oh God . . . Oh God . . . Oh God . . .

(He waits. Nothing happens. He gives up. He finds the pills sitting in front of him, picks them up and hurls them over the gate into the prison, defiantly. He kicks the gate, fights with it, then lets out a sort of intense guttural sigh, falling to his hands and knees, on the edge. He slumps back against the gate, holding the bars with his hands.)

How to Draw Mystical Creatures
By Ellen Margolis

Jamey: age twenty-five, a loving young man

Dramatic

> *Jamey is a young father whose wife and infant son have disappeared. In this scene, he confronts the manager of a family-themed pizza parlor.*

JAMEY: No, I'm not "dining with you." I can't come in, see, because my wife is gone and my kid is gone, and I know that, I know I can't come in. But I can stand outside in case they come out. In case they come out. And it's a good thing I'm here tonight because your employee here — who won't tell me his name, by the way — is not doing his job. He's supposed to be checking their hands, right, and the parents' hands, right, and making sure the kids get home safe and sound. He's just standing here. He doesn't care what happens to these kids, and he's not doing his job. LISTEN TO ME. You can't just let these children go drifting out with whoever. Some of them are toddlers, and little tiny kids, and they can't necessarily tell you if they're being kidnapped or something. You shouldn't have some high school kid for minimum wage doing this job. This is important. It's important.

Places Like Home
By Ira Niles Brodsky

Jonnie: mid-twenties, a working-class gay man, somewhat wild and
   HIV positive

Dramatic

> *Jonnie comes in late at night, somewhat drunk and
> disheveled, and explains to his boyfriend Charlie what he's
> been doing that night and why.*

JONNIE: Charlie, what I've been doing is having fun. I've been having
   fun like someone who's alive and doesn't plan on dying anytime
   soon. I've been talking to all kind of crazy guys, cute, little college boys with streaks in their hair and middle-aged bikers with
   too much body hair and a fat gut. Like tonight this guy with an
   eagle tattoo and pierced nipples. And it turns out that that's not
   all that's pierced. And we get wasted and we listen to music and
   nobody's asking about my test results or whether I took my
   meds. They don't think, "Shit, I'm talking to a dying man." They
   don't even know they're talking to a dying man. We're just brag-
   ging and bullshitting each other and sometimes jerking off in the
   park. It's not great, but at least I feel like I'm alive. You look at
   me, Charlie, and you see a disease, a time bomb waiting to
   explode. But when I go out to the bars, I can leave all that
   behind. I'm sorry that hurts you, but I don't know how long I
   have left, and I figure I deserve a little fun. When I'm gone, you'll
   find somebody better.

Tautology
By Julius Galacki

Son (a.k.a. Randy): late teens, a person who is nonexistent to most people around him; alternately detached and hostile; sensitive, complex, and vastly immature.

Dramatic

> Tautology *is a direct-audience address, monologue play for four characters. In previous monologues, the Son has explained to the audience that he has his mother's name, has revealed the secrets of his imaginary inventions to them, has exulted on his crush on a flag twirler, has lamented about how he doesn't fit in at school, and for that, has been sent to the school shrink. His working-class father, in his monologues, has expressed his frustration and bafflement with his son, as well as his love for his deceased wife who gave him his only years of happiness.*

SON: I'm going to kill my father. I thought about it. We have a long kitchen knife. Through his back into his heart. I'd have to strike really hard. . . . You see I was listening to the birds. I wasn't bothering him! He said how could I listen to the birds for hours. He didn't even look at them. They were little babies jumping from branch to branch. And they sang. Sang. Then he hit them with a stick. I heard the tree try to catch them as they fell. But they were dead already and they couldn't hold back. So they just fell. Then he turned to look at me. I thought he was going to kill me too. That's when I saw her. I hadn't seen her for years. Right then I could feel her brown curls — how much I loved her. How well she took care of me. I knew he was going to kill me, so I screamed "Momma, save me!" And he froze. He started to cry, ran back into the house. She saved me. I've never seen anyone make him cry.

Sacrifices
By Barbara Lhota and Janet B. Milstein

Jay: a young adult, a former gang member and current prisoner

Dramatic

> *Jay, a prisoner put away for a gang-related drug-deal shoot-ing, tells his sister that he cannot forgive their abusive father even if their father has found God.*

JAY: I knew it! Of course *now* he turned to God so he can be forgiven for his sins. *(Beat.)* Wait a minute. You don't expect me to forgive him, do you? Just because he's dying? *(Stacey doesn't speak.)* Oh man! You've got to be kidding me? Forgive and for-get, is that it? Well, I won't forgive. Because I can't forget. Every night I dream — the screams, the torture, the thrown furniture, the broken bones and bruises. I dream about it. I try to stay awake so I won't dream, but I can't. I scream in my sleep. Man, I've scared the other inmates. I dream about your bruised face on Halloween. And watching Mom's glasses shatter one night and hiding under my bed with the wires digging straight into my back because I was so terrified of him. You know! How do you forget these things?! How?! How do you forget them all? *(Beat.)* Where do you put them? Where? Because I've tried that. But they don't stay put away.

Knee Deep in Fish
By Kevin Schwendeman

Jonathan: twenty-six, lawyer, normally grounded and thinking
   there is logic to everything

Dramatic

> *Workaholic Jonathan, a lawyer, meets with his alcoholic
> girlfriend, Anne, for the first time since she left him. Forced
> to be alone, Jonathan struggles to come to terms with his
> own demons and with his love for Anne. With no one to
> speak to besides their pet fish, Jonathan has started to lose
> some sense of reality and buries himself in his work. Here,
> Anne has come to "check on the fish," secretly hoping that
> maybe his time alone will help Jonathan realize what their
> relationship means to him. Anne becomes incredulous when
> she finds that Jonathan has not changed at all and laughs at
> him. This laughter breaks the fragile hold Jonathan has on
> his self-control finally pushing him over the edge.*

JONATHAN: Are you gonna let me in on the joke? Yes! The joke! The
   goddamn joke! Why when I wake up I realize that I was never
   sleeping! No lofty feeling. No rapid eye movement. No dreams.
   Just me and my closet. I can't help but laugh at it. What's the
   joke? Anne! I . . . can't . . . sleep. *(Silence.)*
       I got into bed last week, and I forgot to close the closet door.
   I stared at the closet for hours. The moon was shining through
   the window. There weren't any shadows, Anne. It was just a
   huge singularity . . . a giant black hole that sucked everything in.
   During the day happy clothes. During the night nothing. It just
   sucks the mind dry. But that's not the end of it. There's someone
   in there. He watches me. I can't see him but he's still there. I stare
   at him and wonder who will break first. Then he laughs. He guf-
   faws . . . heartily. So, I laugh. What is it? What's the joke?
   Where's the punch line? What is it? He won't tell me. He
   doesn't talk. He stares and laughs and wears my clothes and
   steals from me. I'm missing my briefcase! Just gone one day. The
   closet took it. He has it . . . he has everything! I just want to
   know what's so funny!

Feast
By Aline Lathrop

Billy: twenty-three, the good son, has spent his life trying to make
up for his father's shortcomings

Dramatic

*Billy's father abandoned the family when Billy and his twin
sister were born. He's always dreamed of being part of a sta-
ble family. Billy has brought his new wife, Nina, home to
meet the family for Thanksgiving. However, the visit forces
Billy to face the turmoil in which his family exists and deep-
ens his fear that he is incapable of being a good husband or
father. He speaks to Nina, who is desperate to start a family with him, on the front stoop of the house.*

BILLY: Look at them. They're falling apart. But I don't begin to pick
up the pieces. Sure, I show up for Thanksgiving, and clean up the
broken vase my mom hurled, but that doesn't make my
family any less broken. And I'll be cruising out of here on Sunday morning. My recipe for success has a lot more to do with
taking what I can for myself and leaving the people in my life
behind. If it didn't, I'd never have gotten this far.

I was thinking about how badly I wanted to start fresh with
you. Ever since I was a kid, I used to dream about finding the
right woman and settling down and becoming someone's father.
And here I am. I've found the right woman. It's all ahead of me
now.

And I do want to be a father. It's just . . . I don't know.
I've always known I wasn't good enough for this.

I Didn't Know You Could Cook
By Rich Orloff

Jerome: twenties

Dramatic

Jerome, a schoolteacher in a wheelchair, has just admitted he's gay to his judgmental older brother.

JEROME: To be honest, after the accident, I wasn't sure what I'd be able to do. At the rehab center, they didn't deal with our sexuality at all. At all. Then about six months later, I — I was watching this Mel Gibson movie, and he started getting real sweaty, and inside I started getting real excited, and outside I got real excited, too . . . I know you're shocked that I'm turned on by Mel Gibson. But then, I'm shocked when I meet someone who isn't . . . And the women, the women were, oh, I don't know. I guess, I guess they were an experiment. I mean, I thought I might be gay even before the accident; actually, I was pretty sure of it. Still, I kept thinking, "Maybe if I meet the right woman . . ." Hell, most of the time the only way I could get it up with them was if I fantasized I was with Mel or . . . Look, damn it, I'm disabled and I'm gay, and that's the way it is, whether you like it or not or I like it or not or anybody in the world likes it or not. I didn't ask to be either. I always figured I'd get married someday and I'd walk down the aisle, and surprise, I'm not going to do either. I know I should be proud that I'm gay, and accepting that I'm disabled, and I suppose I am, but damn it, I've sure had to give up a lot of fantasies, a whole truckload of fantasies.

Elmo on the Half Shell
By Christopher Wall

Joey: twenties, troubled, abusive

Dramatic

> *Joey's hurt his girlfriend, Sue, and he's trying to smooth things over. The problem, you see, isn't with him. It's with his brother, Nate, and the broken home he came from. As Sue listens, doubtfully, Joey reveals for the first time how a neighborhood fight got out of control.*

JOEY: I slapped him. Saw the spray come off his lips. Grabbed the back of his shirt. Pushed him over the guard rail. Kicked him in the head. Above his right temple. With those steel-toed boots I loved so much. I'd never done this before. I mean, not this. But it had its own momentum, you know? I reached down and grabbed something. His hair. And dragged him to the bridge. Why? I've wondered for years. I wish I could come up with a reason. A big reason that makes sense of it all. But the honest truth? It's cause he whimpered. Cause he was fat. And glanced at me the wrong way. Cause I was walking up a hill to meet our starving dog who was eating our starving plants cause no one had the time or the money or, or desire to look after him. I let Sam hang over the railing. Head first. Squealing. This horrible sound. Like an animal. Then, as he reached up, grabbed at my shirt, face beet red, mouth sputtering, saliva, tears, and sweat dripping off his face, I let go. It was a small movement. Like that. My fingers moved an inch. And I watched him fall. Watched his head bob up and down. Saw his blood stain the water. Hair, bone, dandruff, everything — everything just kind of falling out and drifting away and — and suddenly there was my brother shooting BBs in the woods. And Ma falling down the stairs, trying to answer the door to get the flowers I'd sent her. Cause I was trying to make up for things. . . . Why? You're asking me why!? I don't know how any of it got that way!

Elmo on the Half Shell
By Christopher Wall

Joey: twenties, troubled, abusive

Dramatic

> *Joey's hurt his girlfriend, Sue, and he's trying to smooth things over. The problem, you see, isn't with him. It's with his brother, Nate, and the broken home he grew up in. As Sue listens, doubtfully, Joey describes the last time he saw Nate and how the smallest thing, like mentioning his brother's name, can lead to a disturbing outburst.*

JOEY: So — Like I said, I'm at (my brother) Nate's barbecue last year. Paper plate in one hand. Spoonful of coleslaw in the other. Minding my own business. And he turns to me and says, "How's the cripple?" Three words. "How's the cripple?" And the guests who knew (what I did to Sammy) looked at me, and the rest who didn't looked at me. I was trying to have dinner. Spend a holiday with what's left of the family. But the questions were already forming in Laura's mind. They started on the way home. She didn't wait long for the answer. *(Laughs.)* What timing! Me, with a promotion. Apartment. Some good furniture. And what I thought was this beautiful, understanding woman. To rip off a man's shell with a pair of pliers. Expose him in public. It's cruel. It's deadly, you know? My brother won't let me forget. He keeps taking people away. Even when we're not speaking. A year later. In my own pad. Like a fucking magician. *(Pause.)* So. When you told me last week that my brother called. And told me a second time, and a third time, and started asking questions — I lost control. I admit that. And I hit you. Now you know why. I was saving us. I was preserving our future. You have to understand. I'll do anything to keep us together. That's not a bad thing. I don't know how many chances you get to rebuild your life, but I feel like I'm running out, you know?

ACCEPTANCE LETTER by Barbara Lhota and Janet B. Milstein. ©2003 by Barbara Lhota and Janet B. Milstein. Reprinted by permission of the authors. Originally published in *Forensics Series Volume 2, Duo Practice and Performance: 35 8-10 Minute Original Dramatic Plays.* All inquiries should be directed to Barbara Lhota at blhota@aol.com and to Janet B. Milstein at act4you@msn.com, monologues@msn.com

AN ACTOR PREPARES by Mark Young. ©2002 by Mark Young. Reprinted by permission of the author. All inquiries should be addressed to Young2125@comcast.net

THE AGE OF CYNICISM OR KARAOKE NIGHT AT THE HOG by Keith Huff. ©2003 by Keith Huff. Reprinted by permission of the author. All inquiries should be addressed to Huffkeith@aol.com

AGUINALDO: MARK TWAIN IN PURGATORY by Elaine M. Hazzard. ©1994/2004 by Elaine M. Hazzard. Reprinted by permission of the author. All inquiries should be addressed to Elaine M. Hazzard, Attorney At Law, 851 West End Avenue #6F, New York, NY 10025.

AL CAPONE AND ME by Ruth Tyndall Baker. ©2004 by Ruth Tyndall Baker. Reprinted by permission of the author. All inquiries should be addressed to 743 Growth Ave., Ft. Wayne, IN 46808.

ALL THINGS CHICKEN by Julius Galacki. ©1997/2004 by Julius Galacki. Reprinted by permission of the author. All inquiries should be addressed to julius.galacki@aya.yale.edu

ATHEIST COMEDY by Ron Riekki. ©2003 by Ron Riekki. Reprinted by permission of the author. All inquiries should be addressed to ronriekki@hotmail.com

BACK TO SCHOOL by Barbara Lhota and Janet B. Milstein. ©2003 by Barbara Lhota and Janet B. Milstein. Reprinted by permission of the authors. Originally published in *Forensics Series Volume 1, Duo Practice and Competition: 35 8-10 Minute Original Comedic Plays.* All inquiries should be directed to Barbara Lhota at blhota@aol.com and to Janet B. Milstein at act4you@msn.com, monologues@msn.com

BATS by N. M. Brewka. ©2004 by N. M. Brewka. Reprinted by permission of the author. All inquiries should be addressed to clarx@shore.net

BIRDSEND by Keith Huff. ©2002 by Keith Huff. Reprinted by permission of the author. All inquiries should be addressed to Huffkeith@aol.com

BLACK & WHITE by Mark Young. ©2002 by Mark Young. Reprinted by permission of the author. All inquiries should be addressed to Young2125@comcast.net

BRING BACK PETER PAUL RUBENS by Barbara Lhota and Janet B. Milstein. ©2003 by Barbara Lhota and Janet B. Milstein. Reprinted by permission of the authors. Originally published in *Forensics Series Volume 2, Duo Practice and Performance: 35 8-10 Minute Original Dramatic Plays.* All inquiries should be directed to Barbara Lhota at

permission of the author. All inquiries should be addressed to dan@alarmclocktheatre.org

THE LEASH OF THE RAINBOW'S MEOW by Kevin M. Lottes. ©2004 by Kevin M. Lottes. Reprinted by permission of the author. All inquiries should be addressed to Kevin M. Lottes, *barehanded books*, P.O. Box 508, Westerville, OH 43086; 614-783-8702; kevin@barehanded-books.com; www.barehandedbooks.com

LEAVE by Matthew A. Everett. ©1999 by Matthew A. Everett. Reprinted by permission of the author. All inquiries should be addressed to mail@matthewaeverett.com, www.matthewaeverett.com

LIMPING TOWARDS BABYLON by Julius Galacki. ©1997/2005 by Julius Galacki. Reprinted by permission of the author. All inquiries should be addressed to julius.galacki@aya.yale.edu

LIVES OF THE FORMERLY FRENCH by Lauren D. Yee. ©2002 by Lauren D. Yee. Reprinted by permission of the author. All inquiries should be addressed to laurendyee@hotmail.com

LONE STAR GRACE by Suzanne Bradbeer. ©2002 by Suzanne Bradbeer. Reprinted by permission of the author. All inquiries should be addressed to suzannebradbeer@aol.com

MACKENZIE by John Michael Manship. ©2004 by John Michael Manship. Reprinted by permission of the author. All inquiries should be addressed to 471 Medford St., Somerville, MA 02145; E-mail: mike@southcitytheatre.org

MAMA, MADDY AND THE CUCKOO by Dylan Guy. ©1984 by Dylan Guy. Reprinted by permission of the author. All inquiries should be addressed to 233 E. 21st. St. #21, New York, NY 10010; E-mail: Dylan_Guy1@yahoo.com

MARS NEEDS WOMEN, BUT NOT AS MUCH AS ARNOLD SCHECTER by Rich Orloff. ©2004 by Rich Orloff. Reprinted by permission of Playscripts, Inc., which has published the entire text in an acting edition. Contact: Playscripts, Inc., Box 237060, New York, NY 10023, 1-866-NEW-PLAY, www.playscripts.com

MOVING PICTURE by Dan O'Brien. ©2001 by Dan O'Brien. Reprinted by permission of the author. All inquiries should be addressed to Beth Blickers, Abrams Artists Agency, 275 Seventh Avenue, 26th Floor, New York, NY 10001. Phone: 646-486-4600 x222. Fax: 646-486-2358. Beth.Blickers@abramsartist.com

OCTOBER ROSE by Terri Campion. ©2003 by Terri Campion. Reprinted by permission of the author. All inquiries should be addressed to tarriecamp@aol.com

PERSONALLY SPEAKING by Barbara Lhota and Janet B. Milstein. ©2003 by Barbara Lhota and Janet B. Milstein. Reprinted by permission of the authors. Originally published in *Forensics Series Volume 1, Duo Practice and Competition: 35 8-10 Minute Original Comedic Plays*. All inquiries should be directed to Barbara Lhota at blhota@aol.com and to Janet B. Milstein at act4you@msn.com, monologues@msn.com